Working with child sexual abuse

A post-Cleveland guide to effective principles and practice

Open University Press
Milton Keynes · Philadelphia

To Morwenna Toleman, Dorothy Whitaker and Charlotte Lodge, three great social work educators

Open University Press
12 Cofferidge Close
Stony Stratford
Milton Keynes MK11 1BY

and
242 Cherry Street
Philadelphia, PA 19106, USA

First Published 1989

British Library Cataloguing in Publication Data

O'Hagan, Kieran
  Working with child sexual abuse: a
  post-Cleveland guide to effective principles
  and practice
  1. Great Britain. Children. Sexual abuse by adults
  I. Title
  362.7'044

  ISBN 0–335–15598–7
      0–335–15597–9 (paper)

Library of Congress catalog number available

Typeset by Scarborough Typesetting Services
Printed in Great Britain by Alden Press, Oxford

Contents

Acknowledgements

There are two principal groups of contributors to this publication to whom I remain indebted: firstly, those many very young children subjected to the obscenity and degradations of sexual abuse. They may never know about their contribution, but it is immeasurable nonetheless, and the very least they deserve are my strenuous efforts throughout the book to retain their anonymity. I am confident that I have done so. Secondly, to the staff of Harlech Road Divisional Office in South Leeds, many of whom have shared with me past and present experiences of child sexual abuse work. Finally, but by no means least, my thanks to Susan Dobson, whose professional and secretarial excellence transformed my microscopic scribblings into the tables and charts which appear throughout.

1
Prologue: for the protection of the child

It was on a Friday afternoon. The headteacher of a nearby primary school rang. She gave me a referral about one of her children. She spoke in a calm orderly kind of way, but I could sense her underlying anxiety. I too felt anxious; it was a child sexual-abuse referral she was giving me. I discussed it with my senior. We anticipated the worst. Where could we place the child then? He would make enquiries while I investigated. It would have to happen on a Friday afternoon, wouldn't it?

At the school I was introduced to Mrs Woods, the headteacher, Mrs Shaw, the class teacher, and to Ms Greer, a community schools nurse. All three of them had recently been instructed about the behavioural indicators of child sexual abuse. Mrs Shaw had observed a number of these indicators in the behaviour of one of her pupils, Sarah Williams, aged six and a half. Sarah had become rather withdrawn during the past few weeks. She drew pictures of adults in intimate relationships. She had become clingy towards Mrs Shaw. She seemed far less inclined than other children to leave the classroom at the end of the lessons. And Mrs Shaw had noticed an apparent discomfort in the child's face each time she returned from the toilet. Mrs Woods and Mrs Shaw had tried to talk to Sarah, 'Just like good friends', they said. They made some progress in getting the child to admit to the pain she was enduring, but, when they attempted to explore the causes, the child simply clammed up. So they sought help from Ms Greer the community schools nurse who visited the school regularly; she advised them to contact Social Services immediately. No doubt, my arrival was a source of reassurance to them. It wasn't only the convenience of getting rid of a potentially serious child-abuse case on a Friday afternoon, but also their mistaken belief – or misguided hope – that I was much more confident and knowledgeable in dealing with such cases than they were. I made no attempt to enlighten them.

I met Sarah, a beautiful but sad child. How inhibiting it must have been to be brought face to face with four towering adults – even nice friendly ones, which we undoubtedly were. I think we all sensed how inhibiting it must have been, but nobody was displaying any willingness to be left out of the action. Thus we all made an effort to reassure Sarah, commenting on things like her lovely curly hair and her spotted dress, and enquiring what she had been doing in class (before being summoned from the classroom!), etc. Sarah sensed that this was some kind of charade and became far more anxious. But it was convenient for me, as it diverted attention away from my own difficulty in saying that I needed some privacy to speak to the child.

Anatomical dolls are a great source of curiosity to anyone who has never seen them. I didn't have all that much experience in using them, but I was conscious of three pairs of adult eyes fixed upon them, and every move I was making with them. It is normally difficult to stimulate an abused child's interest in the dolls in wholly artificial circumstances like these, but to attempt to do it in front of an audience that has in the previous few minutes induced a high anxiety state in the child is exceptionally difficult. It can also be amusing, however, with the child occasionally glancing up at the professionals' riveting stares and embarrassing silence. I have never felt entirely happy about using the dolls. When the child sees the genitalia for the first time, I have often experienced a vague discomfort. I am not sure why. I can recall many occasions when I have been grateful for the dolls' enabling me to expose varying kinds of abuse. Perhaps it's the occasional absence of the child's mother which makes me uneasy, the fact that she is unaware of what is taking place, and that she may have the strongest objections. Another reason, I think, is that the use of anatomical dolls is a form of manipulation. I am concealing my real motivation from the child whom I am compelling to act in a certain way (i.e. exposing him or her to models of genitalia in the hope that they will talk about the memories these evoke).

The dolls certainly did evoke memories. Sarah demonstrated that she was familiar with the male genitalia, and that she had been sexually abused. She eventually told me her father had 'done it', i.e. engaged her in oral and manual masturbation, digital penetration, and shown her hard-core pornographic literature. Mrs Woods reminded me that Sarah had a younger sister, Elizabeth, aged five, in another class. She was summoned too, and the whole procedure gone over again. Elizabeth did not respond to the dolls, nor did she disclose anything. I was convinced that only Sarah had been abused.

I contacted my senior and informed him. Another colleague, Pat, was sent to meet me at the school. As expected, we were told to visit the children's home. Our purpose was to inform mother of our 'professional concern' and 'invite' her to accompany the children for a paediatric examination. In reality, that meant compelling mother to accept our invitation, by making it clear that she had no option. (She had but, in the interests of the child at this particularly difficult moment, we were not likely to inform her.) We left the children at the school and instructed Mrs Shaw that they remain there until our return. I cautioned her that it was not beyond the bounds of possibility that either Mr or Mrs Williams would make a lightning visit to the school to remove the children as soon as they heard of our investigation.

We left the school and made our way through a sprawling council estate that we both knew so well. The fact that our work in this estate was becoming increasingly dominated by child sexual abuse did not increase our confidence one little bit. It was the type of visit that we both detested, and it showed.

Mrs Williams was devastated by our visit, and Mr Williams, thank God, wasn't there. She was a tallish woman, with a fresh unblemished complexion, and serious dark eyes. Her features seemed solid, strong, sincere. She would have looked invulnerable before we arrived, but our reason for visiting her reduced her to a crumbling heap. We physically restrained her, tried to comfort her and help her to prepare for the journey. We got away, luckily before Mr Williams got back.

Mrs Williams's reaction to her children at the school was disappointingly strange. She rushed towards them, but not to embrace them. There was no love or warmth in her looks, no sighs of relief, no impulse to reassure them. Instead, it was a look that gradually changed from fear and apprehension to something near disgust. Whatever it was, it was conspicuously directed towards Sarah who seemed far less surprised or affected by it than her audience. And it has to be admitted, it served a useful purpose in stabilizing Mrs Williams.

If the school setting seemed conveniently far away from a strange home and family situation, then a million miles further was the shiny new, technologically equipped paediatric clinic. Here children and panic-stricken parents, social workers and police officers daily dropped in, seeking what everyone regards as the crucial opinion of the paediatrician. In this setting the anxieties and fears of parents never change, but the frequency with which all the professionals congregate in the corridors, awaiting the outcome, ensure that their sensitivities and vigilance certainly do change, but not for the better. This is a professional vulnerability to which very few of us do not succumb. And so I have to admit that I occasionally forgot about Mrs Williams's feelings, as I frequently became engaged with the numerous professionals toing and froing for the duration of our visit. It couldn't have been much sense or fun either for the children who never left their mother for a moment.

The procedures for paediatric examination were well established by this time: the detailed questioning of the mother, the paediatrician's own use of the anatomical dolls, the most thorough medical examination, designed to expose *any* type and degree of abuse, and finally the photographic record. Mrs Williams's permission was not sought for any of this. She would have given it, without question, but not willingly; more so because like nearly every other parent taken there, she was simply overwhelmed by the authority and prestige of the place. She was also very frightened.

I watched Mrs Williams throughout the examination. The paediatrician told her that he would have to take some photographs. She resented it, but she was incapable of resisting it and, when she saw her children being directed to pose in what must have appeared to her to be the most sexually explicit manner, for the benefit of his camera, she tried to conceal her shame and disgust, and tried to control her increasing trembling, by clenching her fists and biting hard into her lips. I suddenly thought – a horrible thought, that maybe Mrs Williams was actually thinking that her child was responsible for the abuse, that she had encouraged her father in some way, by posing as she was being asked to do now. It is not uncommon for mothers to believe that their children are responsible, and it was noticeable that Mrs Williams's already unfriendly attitude towards her daughter hardened considerably.

Mrs Williams surely must have felt that we had deceived her. In the school we had comforted her and reassured her that she would 'feel much better' for having visited this place and having permitted her child to be examined by an expert. We had purposely avoided giving her any indication of how detailed and explicit this examination would be; even more so did we avoid mention of the camera, which we knew had become the standard tool for all child sexual-abuse examinations. My colleagues and I have discussed these paediatric examinations on many occasions. I have often pondered the feelings and the experiences of the young children who are increasingly being subjected to them. As I watched Sarah and Elizabeth obediently strip and spread-eagle themselves for the vaginal photography and then double up for the anal, I wondered what exactly did they see, hear, feel, and think? What will they think and feel about it tomorrow, I then asked; next week, next year? How would they remember it when in their teens and adult life? Will it have any effect? any long-term consequences? There is another aspect of these examinations which has often bothered me. Only a male paediatrician could position himself and his camera inches away from the child's vagina and anus whilst he clicks and clicks – any other man would be hauled before the courts on a charge of gross indecency. I have always accepted the necessity of such an examination; I have even admired the systematic rigour with which it is carried out. But on occasions like this, I can never avoid the recurring thought that the mechanics of it bear a striking similarity to numerous categories of criminal child sexual-abuse acts. I am sure that if Mrs Williams had been able to articulate her thoughts on the matter, that is what she might have said. I sympathized with her and felt guilty about her. She had been given no preparation for this ordeal, an 'ordeal' we had known all along that it was going to be.

The paediatrician confirmed that there had 'probably' been some fingering of Sarah's vagina. There was no indication of either vaginal and anal intercourse in either girl. He tried to get a verbal disclosure from Sarah, but by this time she simply wasn't able to give it. She was looking increasingly miserable and forlorn. I telephoned the doctor's confirmation to my senior. He informed the police. He requested them to hold off until such times as I could ascertain whether or not mother was going to co-operate. This meant finding out whether she was willing to accept that her husband had abused Sarah and would accept the necessity of his removal? I soon found out: Mrs Williams was not going to 'co-operate'.

Two police officers arrived at the hospital and interviewed Sarah and her mother once again. Sarah told them nothing; she was too disoriented to give them any response at all. Mrs Williams didn't help; it seemed as though the involvement of the police and their questioning of her were to be the last straw. Nevertheless, the police listened carefully to my own testimony, spoke to the paediatrician, and left to find Mr Williams. I then had the unpleasant task of telling Mrs Williams that I would be seeking a place-of-safety order, and that the children would be removed from her until the allegations had been thoroughly investigated. She broke down and wept hysterically, whilst her two now very confused and tired children became increasingly distraught. The most painful aspect of this scene was that neither mother nor children could reach out to each other in their distress. All three seemed devastated, overwhelmed, in different ways; each conscious of the enormity of the trauma the other was suffering, yet each incapable of consoling each other. Elizabeth surrendered in her effort to stop her mother from crying and simply cried with her, like a helpless puppy. Sarah, however, seemed too dazed to cry. She held one hand upon her mother's stooping shoulder as if to gesture her willingness to help, but she more often stared at me beseechingly, as if she still hoped I might rescue her from all this misery.

Pat and I stood watching awkwardly. We both realized that any attempt to rescue Mrs Williams or comfort her would have been as much deceitful as hypocritical. But our sense of helplessness made us do precisely that, and so we put our arms around her and ignored our own consciences by talking soothingly to her, assuring her that 'we know what this must be like for you . . . this is always the worst part . . . it will turn out all right in the end . . . for you and the kids . . . etc.' (All our experiences of child sexual abuse told us the opposite.)

It was not just our sense of helplessness, of course, nor a lack of courage which made us behave in this way. We needed Mrs Williams. We needed her to recover quickly, so that she could minimize the trauma her children might endure in being separated from her. We needed her to understand why we were acting in the way we were, and to let her children see – or to pretend – that she approved. And above all else, we needed some co-operation from her to avoid highly conflictual and emotional scenes most distressing to ourselves.

We brought Mrs Williams and her children to the Social Services office, and left the children in the company of our colleagues. We then ac-companied Mrs Williams home to collect the children's clothing and essentials, and to face Mr Williams if he was there. He was there, and to our immense relief, so too were the police. Mrs Williams looked mortified but, when she also noticed neighbours' peering eyes behind curtains, and passers-by staring at my own car driving up close behind the police panda, she couldn't get out of the car and into her own home quickly enough. She burst into tears again as she entered the living room. Mr Williams sat in what appeared to be his usual armchair, facing a plain-clothes officer sitting opposite him, and another, standing nearby. He was a tall man, with neatly combed, black, wavy and curly hair. His blue eyes and his relaxed mouth gave nothing away. He was uneducated, unrefined, but he was not unclever, nor inarticulate. Words and whole sentences flowed easily, leading I presume to the irritation and glumness on the faces of the two officers. The difficulty Mr Williams was causing was far greater than that of merely denying the abuse; he gave the very convincing impression that he didn't take any of us or the allegations seriously. That was until we informed him of our intention to remove the children. He exploded then and had to be restrained by the officers. He didn't abuse us verbally. He merely reiterated how preposterous it all was, and how foolish we would be made to look. I would have preferred it if he had cursed us.

Mrs Williams abused us. She seemed inspired by her husband and condemned us as she must have wanted to condemn us when her husband wasn't there. She refused to go with us, not surprisingly, but it nevertheless caused me to fall headlong into one of the commonest pitfalls: instead of accepting that refusal, I tried convincing her how helpful it would be for her children; how much they would appreciate her presence in going to a foster home, and how much more difficult and potentially damaging for them it would be if she did not come. I really meant that, but I should have realized the increasing incredulity in the expressions of both of them. I eventually did, but only when it was too late.

'What do you take me for?' she screamed. 'You want me to make your filthy work easier . . . you want me to help you bust up my home and family . . .'

'No, no, no . . .' I spluttered pathetically, 'that's not . . .', as if it made any difference what I said then. With a fine sense of drama and triumph they then ignored me. It was time to go.

I would have been glad to have encountered any diversionary problem after that humiliation. A major one was looming when we got back to the office. Despite valiant efforts, my seniors had been unable to pacify two increasingly unhappy and distressed children, nor had they made any progress in finding a suitable fostering placement. Worse was to follow, because the children immediately perceived our return as confirmation that they were going to be reunited with their parents. We were both taken aback by the fact that Sarah wanted to be reunited just as much as Elizabeth did. And when we attempted to stall her on her ceaseless enquiry to know when they would be reunited, she sensed what our intentions really were and demanded that she and Elizabeth be taken home to their mum immediately. That defiant demand was accompanied by painful, fearful tears, which worried me, and when she stared straight into my own eyes and 'warned' me that 'she would tell her mummy and daddy' what I was doing, I felt so miserable and confused that I almost replied 'Please tell me.' Was this really the child who had disclosed to me a few hours before the revolting sexual abuse to which she'd been subjected?

We eventually found foster parents willing to have the children. Only on condition, however, that it would be for no more than a few days. That would surely mean another fostering then, or residential care. But it didn't matter too much to me at this moment, as I was extremely grateful for any kind of movement. I was beginning to feel physically exhausted and emotionally drained, and it must have been this exhaustion which helped me overcome the discomforting realization that I was placing children in a foster home in the most unprofessional and unethical way that I could have imagined. I had to pretend, however, to the children, and to my colleagues, and to the foster parents, that I believed precisely the opposite; that I knew exactly what I was doing and was wholly confident that it was the right thing to do. Intellectually and verbally this pretence was possible. But emotionally I just felt sick.

And so, at 7.45 p.m. on a Friday evening, I delivered two extremely unhappy children to a foster home. The foster parents didn't want these children; they had merely caved in to the pressure which we had applied. That did not mean that they would be bad foster parents. On the contrary, they had fostered successfully for our department for years. But what it did mean was something I dreaded, yet something predictable and inevitable: that they would indulge in (the usually harmless) banter about social workers not having a clue about what they were doing, and over-used, underpaid foster parents like themselves always having to bail them out, particularly on a Friday evening.

It was not therefore the most pleasant journey homewards. Exhausted I might have been, but my mind was in a state of turmoil. I repeatedly asked myself how had this situation come about, how could I have inflicted so much pain and distress on children, one of whom, I was convinced, had been seriously sexually abused. There was another memory that disturbed me. It was the way each and every professional had to approach the abused child in such a way that she could never know or understand what it was we wanted from her. The teachers had asked her questions pretending that they merely wanted to 'stay friends with her'; the nurse had pretended that she merely wanted to 'have a look at her'; I had pretended that I wanted to 'play dolls with her'; and the paediatrician had pretended that he merely wanted to 'make her better'. In other words we had perpetrated and sustained a conscious deceit upon the child, had caused her and her sister great misery in the process and had finally severed them from the parents they needed as much as they loved. It was of course all in the interest of *protecting the child*.

I'm sure the abuser too had deceived Sarah many times. I'm sure he had 'pretended' to her that he was only doing many innocent and enjoyable things. But as to which deceit and which consequence had done the greatest harm, I most certainly wasn't sure.

2
Cleveland: the origins and the aftermath

The irony of Cleveland

In the recent British history of intervention in child sexual abuse, the experiences of Sarah and Elizabeth cannot be regarded as either uncommon or extreme. Experienced social workers, paediatricians and police officers will know of far worse fates which might have befallen them, and the public at large are now aware that some of the most prominent groups within the child sexual-abuse industry, somehow, inexplicably, unintentionally, subjected many children and their parents to an institutional and bureaucratic ordeal as damaging, if not more so, than any alleged sexual abuse which the children may have originally been enduring.

It is ironic that the tragedy of Cleveland should have occurred *after* the deluge of literature on child sexual abuse – mainly American, telling everyone what we should know and do about it; *after* the consequential nationwide explosion of interest in the topic; *after* the repetitive media appearances and commissioned articles by this country's most authoritative voices on the topic; *after* the political and moral crusades which were launched for the sole purpose of exposing and eradicating it; *after* the appointments of dozens of child sexual-abuse 'consultants' and child sexual-abuse teams, and the establishment of 'hotlines', 'touchlines', 'lifelines', 'carelines', 'childlines' and rape and incest centres, and, not least, *long after* universal acknowledgement that multi-disciplinary co-operation and mutual respect between agencies was the key to any effective intervention and treatment programme. Cleveland and the forgotten hundreds of similar tragedies in other locations occurred *after* all of these wholly admirable and necessary responses to child sexual abuse.

Is the how and why of Cleveland therefore satisfactorily explained by what now appears to be the obvious? that the professionals' enthusiasm ran amok, that their determination blinded them, and that their rapidly constructed bureaucratic edifices of 'prevention' and 'protection' imperceptibly desensitized and depersonalized them?

A precedent for Cleveland

Should this have been the case, it is not entirely without precedent. Similar developments are easily identifiable in the recent history of child physical abuse. Horrific deaths of children have nearly always led to public enquiries and nationwide media and public interest. The gory details have generated waves of revulsion which have inevitably affected the politicians. A new determination has (repeatedly) been expressed; strict new procedures have been drawn up; new child-abuse appointments have been created; organizational systems have been restructured, and directors of social services have invariably declared that similar tragedies will never occur again! For a while then the most assiduous investigations of physical abuse are carried out, medical examinations for the most inconspicuous bruising, massive interventions, a dramatic increase in place-of-safety orders, case conferences, interim-care orders and, equally inevitably, the eventual realization that social workers, police officers and paediatricians have gone 'way over the top', inflicting as much pain and injury on unharmed children and their innocent parents than any physical abuse or neglect originally referred. It is precedents like these which have led to the establishment of equally necessary parents' rights groups like PAIN (Parents against Injustice (Whitehouse 1986)), and the Family Rights Group (Tunnard 1983).

There is a significant difference, however, between the origins of our responses to the physical and sexual abuse of children. In the former the nature of the abuse and its consequences are crystal clear: a classification of bruising, beating, burning, neglect, torture, starvation and death too painful to contemplate. In the latter there is no such clarity: the professionals, let alone the public, are not even certain what they mean by sexual abuse. They are only beginning to categorize it and research its long-term effects. More conspicuously, there are no sexual-abuse equivalents of murdered children like Maria Colwell or Jasmine Beckford; no battered corpses that would have similarly gripped the nation's conscience, provoked the wrath of the social-work-bashing press and galvanized the politicians into action. And yet sexual abuse did stir the public's conscience; the press did become interested, and the politicians, both local and national, did get involved. It is not difficult to see why: all this concern and involvement was based largely upon the professionals' and the public's perception of child sexual abuse as something infinitely more serious, damaging and disgusting than physical abuse. These perceptions encouraged the formulation of drastic procedures and strategies for responding to it. The experiences of Sarah and Elizabeth in the previous chapter – familiar to most grass-roots police officers, social workers and teachers throughout the country, *not just in Cleveland* – are a direct consequence of the implementation of such procedures and strategies.

The 'convenience' of child sexual abuse

The shift in emphasis and resources which then followed, from the physical to the sexual abuse of children, was inevitable. But, it has to be admitted, it was also convenient. First, the removal of a sexually abused child was less complicated and less difficult than the removal of a physically abused child; the criminality of sexual abuse was much less ambiguous than the criminality of physical abuse. Consequently, place-of-safety orders were easy to obtain when sexual abuse was alleged, and the removal wholeheartedly supported by a horrified punishment-seeking public at large. Second, and more ominously, the removal of an allegedly sexually abused child made it unnecessary and virtually impossible to work with the parents of the child. Professionals generally find it difficult to work with abusing parents of any kind, but they have the deepest reluctance even to attempt to work with sexually abusing parents (Simmons 1986). Third, politicians responded enthusiastically. They approved of and provided public funds for the massive expansion of what in effect became a child sexual-abuse industry. The establishment of 'child sexual-abuse teams' became a much sought-after goal, to be achieved by a number of departments reporting a high incidence of child sexual abuse, e.g. Leeds, Lewisham, Dundee, etc.

'Childwatch'

BBC's 'Childwatch', broadcast in October 1986, accelerated all these developments. Its medium was infinitely more powerful and influential than any textbook. The usual criticisms of similar television programmes on serious social problems can be made of 'Childwatch', i.e. that it was a neatly packaged television presentation without substance; a play upon emotion rather than a rigorous analysis of the problem; that it was opportunistic and self-congratulatory. The main criticism, however, should be directed at the conviction on which the programme was based, one already referred to in this chapter, namely, that child sexual abuse is something worse and far more damaging than any other kind of abuse. This conviction pervaded the whole of 'Childwatch' and was clearly expressed in the following exchange:

Interviewer:
What strikes me with great force is the fear of a child who decides that they want to tell someone, but maybe realizes that as soon as they do, the whole of its world will fall apart . . . the police will be informed . . . social services . . . headmasters, the family will then be blown apart . . . what do you do to allay those fears?

To this crucial question, the deputy director of Childline replied:

> Well, the sort of situation that they're living with from day to day is obviously . . . em . . . quite dreadful for these children already. And although it might be quite frightening for them to think initially of what might happen with strange people coming into their homes, on the long-term basis that is certainly much better than living with the terrible things that they are doing now.

It is obvious that this conviction was a major motivating factor behind the tragedy of Cleveland. When the tragedy became public, we heard and read spokespersons and managers daily claim that they had a paramount duty to rescue children from the horror of child sexual abuse. Eight months before, the presenters, participants and supporters of 'Childwatch' argued and pleaded that every sensible person should do the same. The common conviction was not just that sexual abuse was the worst of all abuses, but that whatever happened to children after they had been rescued from such abuse could only be better. This, of course, merely mirrored the perceptions of the public. The most dubious achievement of 'Childwatch' was to reinforce such perceptions. (It is sobering to reflect upon the number of reputable child sexual-abuse experts and social-services chiefs who participated in the programme, and who were seemingly unaware of how dangerous such perceptions in the minds of determined, well-intentioned professionals would prove to be.)

The front line

If the leaders, the pioneers and the experts were demonstrating this lack of awareness before an audience of some twelve to fifteen million people, what about the 'troops' at the front line, a million miles away from the glamour and the gloss of Lime Grove. Were they similarly enthused by this crusade? As a senior social worker, guardian ad litem and trainer at that time, my job was taking me to various parts of the country. It was something of a relief to find that police officers, social workers and medical personnel were not just unenthusiastic, but that they were expressing cynicism, doubt and even fear. They were, in effect, convinced of the programme's potential for calamitous results.

What precisely were these doubts and fears? Upon what were they based? Generally, front-line staff were apprehensive about the increasingly high profile which the media, and 'Childwatch' in particular, were intentionally affording child sexual abuse. More specifically, they were apprehensive about the dramatic increase in referrals and the lack of resources to cope with them. Management's response, in the form of continually amended policy statements and procedures, was becoming more extreme and more paranoid. Overall, the strategies being devised were as much lacking in coherence and intelligence, as they were rigid and cruel in their effects.

Doubts and fears arose out of observing countless enforced separations of children and their parents, and the placement of children in totally inadequate alternative care. The traumas inflicted were very visible, and the harm done often irreparable. Doubts and fears arose as it was realized that child sexual-abuse case conferences were increasingly dominated by paediatric opinion, a domination often based upon a single medical examination lasting no more than a few minutes. Monumental and disastrous decisions were often made on the basis of such examinations. Doubts and fears arose out of the glaring inadequacy of fostering resources in particular, and the alarming rate of fostering breakdowns involving sexually abused children. The need for alternative and adequate residential care then became paramount, at a time when nearly all social-services departments were vigorously pursuing a policy of closure of their residential facilities. Finally, doubts and fears were shared in the disturbing self-realization of how ill-prepared and untrained professionals were for child sexual-abuse work. The training which eventually came their way was entirely child and abuse centred, ignoring the family and social contexts in which the abuse took place, ignoring perpetrators and what to do with them, ignoring the crucial importance of preparing and supporting foster parents – all this ensuring the continuing lack of knowledge, confidence and techniques necessary to work effectively within these contexts.

It cannot be stressed often enough that this ground swell of grass-roots professional concern was not confined to the geographical and moral climate of Cleveland. I can recall many examples of it elsewhere. A few days after 'Childwatch', a local police sergeant in South Yorkshire was apologizing to me for the 'lightning strike' he and his colleagues had made on a 'dopey', uneducated, harmless youth – a client of mine, whom they had picked up only minutes after a disreputable neighbour had made allegations that he had 'interfered' with a child in the neighbourhood. The officers admitted to me afterwards that they had never believed the neighbour, whom they knew well, but it didn't stop them keeping my client locked up for five hours and repeatedly grilling him. I'm sure the sergeant was speaking for many when he said: 'Sorry . . . new procedures . . . they've gone barmy up there . . .'

Management, literature and training: the realities

An important question arises here. How could management have been unaware of the widespread cynicism, doubt and apprehension of its front-line staff towards the increasingly unsound and unethical policies and strategies which they were devising? But so too must similar questions be addressed to the front-line staff: how was it that they continued to implement these policies and strategies without being able to communicate their daily observations of the disastrous effects? How could they tolerate having no influence on the matter for so long? The answers clearly lie in the political, legal and managerial context of provision for coping with the phenomenal increase in child sexual-abuse referrals. A great deception has been unwittingly perpetrated against the British public during the past few years. Politicians, managers and public figures, together with prominent practitioners in the field, have deceived the public into thinking that the mass exposure of child sexual abuse was progress in itself. Another similar deception was that knowledge and understanding about child sexual abuse – and even more, the ability to articulate that knowledge and understanding – were, in themselves, effective strategies. These deceptions have had two major effects: first, they have diverted attention from major difficulties in the legal and managerial contexts; second, they have determined the nature and content of child sexual-abuse literature and training.

Literature and training for child sexual-abuse work have been entirely child oriented. The social worker in the previous chapter was the recipient of it. If the child Sarah had been an orphan, found wandering the streets, horribly sexually abused by strangers, then how fortunate she would have been, placed in the hands of social workers, whose only (pleasant) task would have been to rescue her and find her the best possible short-term and permanent care. But Sarah was no orphan; she was the child of a complex family, a family in which she was undoubtedly being abused, and yet a family which meant so much to her that her removal from it was felt to be far more traumatic and damaging than remaining. Social workers have never been prepared, either by managers or trainers, for the complexities and dilemmas of situations like these.

The legal context

Whatever the failings of the managers and trainers of the social worker in the previous chapter might have been, they should not detract from a serious flaw in the attitude, as much as in the actions, of that social worker. Such attitudes and actions stemmed from a common assumption that welfare professionals are basically helpless in doing anything constructive in response to child sexual abuse other than rescuing and protecting the child from further abuse. After the 'rescue', a traditionally punitive law takes its course, which is likely to mean a vigorous attempt by the police to prosecute, remand, convict and imprison. These developments are initiated and supervised at various stages by the police, the Crown Prosecution Service, solicitors and the judiciary. Social workers play little or no part in these processes and have virtually no influence on the outcome.

British law pertaining to child sexual abuse is not dissimilar to the laws in many other Western countries and is firmly rooted in the criminalization of child sexual abuse: abusers are criminals who perpetrate a particularly revolting kind of crime, and they must be punished severely. The law and the conviction are supported and shared not just by the vast majority of the public but, equally so, by the vast majority of professionals. It is a justifiable law, morally valid, uncomplicated, yet terribly terribly ineffective, either as a deterrent or in providing adequate care and protection for the sexually abused child. Cleveland has confirmed what many professionals have been thinking in recent times: that no real progress can be made unless the law is substantially amended. Others believe that existing laws simply need to be interpreted more liberally and more imaginatively by the judiciary, particularly in sentencing. Opposition to any change in the law is firmly based upon the conviction that the offender is responsible for the abuse, and that sexually abused children must see that society realizes the gravity of the crime committed against them; hence the severest punishment. The counter-argument, that such law and the punitive motivation underlying it do far more harm than good to the child, provokes another interesting argument, that it is the perpetrator who must accept responsibility not just for the abuse, but for its consequences; if, for example, disclosure results in the (very typical) consequences witnessed in Sarah's case, then so be it, the perpetrator is responsible. However, as was also seen in that case, even though the offender is responsible for consequences that child-care professionals would try desperately to avoid, it is actually the professionals themselves who 'implement' those consequences.

This is all very interesting, but, to go back to the attitude of the social worker in the previous chapter, it is precisely because of the increasingly intensive debate on whether or not the law needs to be changed that there is less attention given to the quality of the initial investigation and intervention. The general view is that, as long as the child is 'rescued' and protected from the abuse and gives a disclosure, one shouldn't expect much more from investigation and intervention; the police are then mainly responsible, and the courts will determine the perpetrator's fate.

Post-Cleveland: the task ahead

A new training, a new literature

Many of the problems in attitude, management and in child sexual-abuse literature and training, have their origins in the pre-Cleveland public and professional panic, and in the means adopted for coping with it. A major reappraisal is taking place. Lecturers, writers, practitioners, 'experts' – even the DHSS – are all being made to scrutinize their own contributions to the thinking and attitudes and practices which led to the Cleveland tragedy (let's not pretend that they *did not* contribute). The turnaround is embarrassing, more so for those authors, trainers and managers caught up and carried along by the events, and laying down so-called principles for the staff and students as they went by; for example, the protection of the child is paramount . . . you must always believe the child . . . nothing can be achieved without the perpetrator's admission . . . you must always intervene to stop child sexual abuse . . . and, the most astonishing and heavily criticized Cleveland memorandum, 'where . . . there is medical evidence of

sexual abuse, an immediate place of safety order should be taken . . .'
(quoted in Butler-Sloss 1988: 65). It is simplistic statements and instructions
like these which, without context or categorization, have caused social
workers to inflict massive damage upon families and the children they
sought to 'protect'; I have not the slightest doubt that there have been many
unpublicized mini-Clevelands as a consequence.

As well as enabling social workers and other professionals to provide a far
higher quality of service than that demonstrated in the previous chapter,
there are therefore two principal 'reversing' goals to be sought in relevant
literature and effective training for child sexual-abuse work: first, social
workers will have to accept that, for far too long now, they have been
encouraged to focus entirely upon the problems and symptoms of the
sexually abused child as a convenient diversion from the task of learning
about and learning how to cope with the social and family life of that child,
particularly with what is felt to be the revolting perpetrator of the abuse.
Child sexual-abuse training for social workers in particular must therefore
be family and community oriented. Second, literature and training must
repeatedly demonstrate that many of the advances already made in working
with the victims in isolation from their family and social contexts do not
constitute an effective treatment programme. On the contrary, success in
communicating and relating to the child can often exacerbate existing
difficulties one is having with those who exert far more influence over the
child.

There are numerous other scrutinies necessary of different aspects of the
inadequate training and literature to which social workers have been
subjected: the research basis of attitudes and interventions preceding
Cleveland; how the topic of perpetrators has been presented, and how that
presentation has actually discouraged social workers even more from
attempting to work with them; why is a fundamentally important and
necessary social-work categorization of child sexual abuse lacking; why has
an effective established framework of response to child abuse generally, i.e.
referral, investigation, intervention and case conference phases, been
dismantled, to be replaced by a near obsessive and disastrous drive towards
'rescue', 'protection' and 'disclosure'; and, what is the reason for the neglect
of foster parents, the most precious child-care resource that social services
possess in trying to cope with child sexual abuse.

New training and literature must not just scrutinize and criticize the old, it
must put something effective in its place. (I hope this text will make a small
contribution.) But even when it does, problems and limitations still arise
from the legal (punitive) context of child sexual abuse. Do professionals
really want to get involved in Sarah's case, for example, if they believe they
have nothing to offer her allegedly offending father other than a lengthy
spell of imprisonment, her mother and both children only a life of penury
and stigma, and, above all else, the inflicting of a debilitating guilt upon
Sarah herself as a consequence? There are two responses to that widespread
and understandable belief: first, irrespective of whatever the legal outcome

of a case, the initial investigation and intervention by social services seeking to protect the child should be of a quality and expertise that will have far-reaching benefits for the overall management of the case, and in preparing the child and non-abusing parent for the subsequent investigation and its consequences. Even if one of those consequences is the removal and eventual imprisonment of the perpetrator, that need not be the disaster which is often predicted; indeed, it may be the only logical and beneficial outcome, to which, depending upon that very quality of investigation and intervention, the non-abusing parent and the child may willingly contribute. Second, the existing law does indeed limit responses and, in certain cases, dictate outcomes which definitely are not in the child's interests. Social workers and managers, therefore, like all other professionals, do have an obligation to identify these cases, to quantify and analyse them, to chart precisely how due legal processes from police investigation through prosecution, trial, verdict and imprisonment (or discharge), can adversely affect the victim, can actually make a mockery of the claim that one is 'protecting' that victim from further abuse. They should take every opportunity to inform the crucial agencies, namely, the police and judiciary, of this possibility. If there is any 'benefit' at all from the massive increase in child sexual-abuse cases, it can only be that it is concentrating the minds of everyone in such a way that they must realize the dangers as well as the opportunities in professional responses and legal processes.

The origins and contents of this particular contribution

Nearly all previous texts on child sexual abuse have been written by acknowledged experts and have been based upon experience and success in varying degrees. I must make two points here; first, I am no expert, and second, I have benefited very little from a substantial reading of the experiences and acknowledged expertise of others. I am a principal caseworker, specializing in child abuse, and working in an inner-city area. The vast bulk of the literature and training for child sexual-abuse work has not been produced either for or by people like myself. It has in the main been produced by American researchers and practitioners who know nothing about British law, social-services departments or British social-work practice. The British contribution to the literature has been increasing, but, rather than demonstrating some awareness and understanding of the harsh realities faced by the social worker in the previous chapter, and producing new insights, frameworks, skills and techniques that might enable social workers to face up to them, it has invariably and increasingly trodden along familiar ideological pathways. The principal goals in many British textbooks and articles seem to be that of convincing readers about the merits of a particular perspective on child sexual abuse, and the demerits of others, plus providing numerous strategies for getting disclosures, and for providing services and therapies for sexually abused children in the absence of their parents. This is not to decry such goals; there are instances when a particular perspective will be the most perceptive one, and there are many instances when children – particularly teenagers – can benefit from therapies which do not include their parents. But the fact remains that such literature has contributed little towards helping social workers in social-services departments in their initial responses to what is a very common yet difficult child sexual-abuse referral, that of Sarah and Elizabeth in the previous chapter. There is nothing so dispiriting for workers reading one of those well-written textbooks which seem to have all the answers as the quick realization that 'all the answers' are available because the authors have neither experience nor understanding of the harsh realities of social-services life.

This book is a product of many years' experience of working in that kind of context. It will repeatedly refer to, describe and face up to its realities. It will express opinion and pursue analysis strictly through the realities of cases, rather than through a philosophical or ideological viewpoint. It will constantly seek to narrow the focus, that is to say that *it definitely is not* a book which will attempt to deal with all aspects of child sexual abuse; on the contrary, it is primarily concerned with identifying that category of case which poses the greatest challenge to social workers. It will then aim to provide a secure foundation, comprehensive frameworks, and some skills and techniques through which social workers and their professional colleagues can at least provide a high quality of service in the crucially significant initial phases of child sexual-abuse work; these are the referral, investigative, intervention and case-conference phases.

Chapter 3 will begin by focusing on a number of paradoxes in the literature on child sexual abuse. This is symptomatic of the infancy of studying the topic, and of the diversity of perceptions of its origins and causes. Current theories, philosophies and practices in child sexual-abuse work will be examined, giving particular attention to the feminist and humanist perspectives, and to the treatment programmes devised by Giarretto (1978, 1981). Chapter 4 will attempt to introduce an ethical dimension and awareness into child sexual abuse (probably most appropriate in the light of events in the first chapter). Chapter 5 will critically review research literature. It will question the relevance of much of this literature and its research findings to the realities of child sexual-abuse tasks for social workers in this country. Chapter 6 will seek to find a meaningful categorization of child sexual abuse, specifically for social workers. Which type of child sexual-abuse case poses the greatest challenge for social workers who have statutory responsibilities in respect of the victims? Chapter 7 will focus upon what is possibly the most formidable challenge for all involved professionals, namely, the perpetrators. The reasons why this is so formidable a challenge will be explored, as will the causes of a probable increase in the number of perpetrators. Strategies for dealing with specific categories of perpetrators will be provided and scrutinized. Chapter 8 will attempt to re-establish the secure foundation upon which effective child sexual-abuse work is based, i.e. a sound ethical base and highly professional

referral-taking, investigating, intervening and case conferences. It will
return to the case of Sarah and Elizabeth and begin again from the
beginning. The secure foundation and the professionalism will be seen to be
effective. Finally, Chapter 9 will look at a much neglected problem: the
fostering of sexually abused children. An effective and tested training course
for foster parents will be described.

Conclusion

We must not deceive ourselves that the Cleveland enquiry report and the
criticisms within it will prevent the kind of experiences described in the first
chapter from occurring again. Cleveland is the child sexual-abuse equivalent
of the Maria Colwell report, both of them supposedly heralding an entirely
different, more professional, more disciplined and far more effective
approach to their respective problem subjects. After some twenty or more
similar Maria Colwell reports, the most damning of which was the Jasmine
Beckford report, there is a justifiable scepticism amongst public and
professionals alike about the usefulness of child-abuse inquiries in general.
This book does not seek to condemn anyone, nor will it dwell upon the
unethical and unprofessional practices exposed by Cleveland. In addition to
the aims already stated however, the following chapters will also focus upon
those characteristics and vulnerabilities of welfare bureaucracies which
clearly have the potential for causing such tragedies again. The principal aim
of the book is to minimize that potential.

3

Literature, perspectives and strategies

Introduction

The volume of child sexual-abuse literature now available suggests that there is no shortage of authority and expertise. But one of the most experienced practitioners cautions: 'beware of "experts" bearing expertise. The field is too new and the body of accumulated knowledge and skills is too small and inadequately tested for anyone to claim that he or she has the answers' (Sgroi 1982a: 6). There are many different aspects of child sexual abuse. There is unlimited scope for researchers writers, practitioners, theorists, and strategists and, more recently, for politicians and public figures. If some cohesion and unanimity had been achieved, then, no doubt, effective policies and practices would have evolved quite rapidly. The reality is, however, that, in the literature, theoretical perspectives and treatment programmes, no such cohesion or unanimity exists. This chapter seeks to probe the reasons for that. It will, first of all, identify some features of the literature which clearly indicate the difficulty writers have in being consistent, knowledgeable and confident about a most complex problem; second, it will classify the literature according to its content and goals; third, it will explore some of the principal perspectives in the literature. Fourth, it will describe a number of treatment programmes which have evolved. And finally, it will suggest that these differing treatments only mirror the crucially important and differing legal and political contexts from which they have emerged.

Paradoxes, confusions and uncertainties

There are some striking paradoxes in child sexual-abuse literature. The authors' first and most important objective is usually to make us aware of the horrific nature and dimensions of child sexual abuse in British and American societies today. This is commonly done by giving the reader numerous statistics, intermittent sample horror stories, and the authors' conviction that the nature and extent of such abuse is worse than those statistics may imply. We cannot doubt then the moral and professional necessity of combating child sexual abuse, nor can we be under any illusion about the size and complexity of the task of combating it effectively. Later, however, we are also likely to be given an historical and cultural perspective (e.g. Schultz 1982) which greatly undermines whatever success has been achieved in telling us how uniquely awful child sexual abuse is: the author will describe far more barbaric sexual abuses of children in ancient times and, worse still, inform us that such abuses were never perceived as such; on the contrary, were – and still are in many non-Western societies – politically, socially and legally quite acceptable.

Most literature dwells at some point upon the traumas involved in child sexual abuse; upon what is believed to be its damaging long-term emotional, sexual, physical and psychological consequences (e.g. Tufts 1984; Bagley and Ramsay 1987; Finkelhor 1986). The same literature, however, will also dwell upon the high prevalence of child sexual abuse, informing us that at least 10 per cent of the adult population has been sexually abused in child-hood – a supposedly 'conservative' estimate by Fontaine (1988), or, as many as 48 per cent, the staggeringly high estimate by Nash and West (1985). Does this mean that between 10 and 48 per cent of the adult population has been damaged in some way, emotionally, sexually, physically or psychologically, as a consequence of being sexually abused during their childhood? The population as a whole may find this difficult to believe.

Perhaps the most frustrating paradox has been generated by the literature itself: its demand for more literature, training and research, and the enthusiastic response to these demands by practitioners, politicians, welfare agencies and their staff. Has the abundance of training and literature equipped front-line staff to cope more professionally and more effectively with the typical child-abuse referral described in Chapter 1? Clearly the answer is not necessarily 'yes'; the Cleveland report may justify a resounding 'no'.

To add to the confusion, we are reminded that the current Western problem of child sexual abuse, in all its numerous and manifest perversions, exists in an era of unparalleled expansion of child-protection services. The extent of child sexual abuse has really nothing to do with that expansion; nor indeed can the expansion take credit for the exposure. The only 'confusing certainty' is that child-protection agencies and the thousands of professionals working in them have had virtually no impact on the dramatic rise in the reported incidence of child sexual abuse.

Understanding and relevance

Paradoxes like these raise serious questions. Could they be indicative of a lack of confidence and an uncertainty in attempting to write about, understand and deal effectively with the problems of child sexual abuse in Britain today? If so, then the cultural and historical contexts of the topic provide a convenient diversion. Thus we may learn plenty about the ancient Roman practices of castrating male babies for homosexual exploitation in their later years (De Mause 1974); the frequency and function of incest amongst the Mohave Indians (Devereaux 1939); the ghastly practice of clitoridectomy carried out throughout the modern Eastern and Western world (Mrazek 1981). Fascinating such cultural and historical titbits may be, but for the average social worker, paediatrician or police officer in Britain today, confronted, for example, with the buggery of a twelve-year-old by his brother in the dingy attic of an inner city slum, or by the digital anal penetration of a two-year-old by its middle-class 'respectable' grandfather, such erudite learning is, quite frankly, irrelevant.

All literature on child sexual abuse has contributed in varying degrees to our understanding. In this practitioner's view, however, very little of the literature is either relevant or helpful in equipping front-line professional staff to cope with the multiple problems created by the abuse. That is no fault of the writers or the researchers, who admirably try to enlighten and inform. The irrelevancy arises out of the novel and fascinating nature of virtually all aspects of child sexual abuse – even the statistics have a compelling quality. 'Training' in child sexual abuse has become synonomous with 'learning' about child sexual abuse. Seldom, if ever, is the reader or trainee encouraged or motivated to pause and ask: of what relevance is this newly acquired understanding to the specific problems I encounter? to the environment in which I operate? to the categories of sexual abuse, victims, and offenders most familiar to me? to the agencies and their personnel with whom I have to liaise?

Such questions may challenge the assumptions of 'relevancy' and 'necessity' about much of the literature and training which have been so much in abundance in recent years (O'Hagan 1988). For example, the problem of what to do with grandfathers who digitally penetrate their two-year-olds is so challenging that it is seldom, if ever, mentioned in the literature. A useful starting point in assessing relevancy to the kind of problems which have been described, is to categorize literature itself. Despite the deluge of articles, textbooks and training cassettes, and the numerous organizational procedures now available, there are still only a handful of types of literary presentation:

1 The victim's experiences, particularly those recorded by the victim. Victims' personal experiences are always relevant to front-line staff. (After Cleveland, we must now also be prepared to read of traumas unwittingly inflicted by protective agencies as much as by abusers.)
2 Perspectives on child sexual abuse. The most relevant perspectives in literature and training are obviously those which have been, or which we think may be, influential in the formulation and implementation of effective policies.

3 Research and statistics. Much research and its emerging statistics are relevant to the tasks faced by front-line staff. Regrettably, much of it is not. (See Chapter 5.)

4 Organizational procedures and guidelines. There is good reason to believe that, in the field of child abuse generally, organizational procedures are very often a knee-jerk reaction to media scrutiny or public opinion. In respect therefore of either understanding or relevance, it is unlikely that any set of procedures is going to satisfactorily enlighten or equip front-line staff. On the other hand, we now know that some procedures have had disastrous repercussions; the questions how and why are highly relevant.

5 Treatment programmes. These are always relevant, as they are usually preceded by a presentation of the philosophy and experiences which underpin their essential components and goals. Furthermore, the fact that they reach the stage of becoming a treatment programme strongly implies that they achieve some degree of success.

6 Skills and techniques. Surprisingly, these may or may not be relevant. There isn't, for example, much point in learning six valuable skills for working with adolescent incest victims, if the vast majority of sexual-abuse cases you encounter consists of children under ten, abused by non-family members. Skills and techniques for interviewing children under five and for facilitating disclosure of sexual abuse with the aid of anatomical dolls are two of the most popular learning areas. These are not likely to help, however, in interviewing adolescent male victims. More pertinent to the question of relevancy is the rather narrow focus of the 'skills and techniques' component. It is wholly child centred and gives little consideration to the more complex task of working with the families of victims, particularly the perpetrators. It can reasonably be argued that success in relating to and in working with children in isolation from the abusing family to which they belong actually exacerbates the difficulties encountered in the task of working with those same families. As yet there is no reputable skills-and-techniques training that would enable social workers to feel confident enough to engage whole families of sexually abused children.

We will now examine two important components in child sexual-abuse literature and training: perspectives and treatment programmes.

Perspectives on child sexual abuse

The feminist perspective

The importance of the feminist perspective is firmly based upon its contribution to the exposure of child sexual abuse, its analysis of the underlying causes and the relevance of feminism's history and literature to the current debate upon how best to respond to the numerous and complex problems associated with it.

Exposure

Child sexual abuse has been exposed principally through research, opinion polls and personal testimony. Research and opinion polls will be scrutinized in a later chapter, but it suffices to say at this stage that they consist in the main of poorly designed studies and limited clinical samples. A more important characteristic (and flaw) is that the cold, bare (and often highly questionable) statistics which emerge in their findings tell us nothing about the nature of child sexual abuse, nor about the emotional, psychological and social repercussions experienced by the victims. Consequently much of the research and opinion polls has been interpreted (and misinterpreted) in various ways, leading to a gathering confusion about the extent and impact of child sexual abuse.

The feminist contribution to the exposure of child sexual abuse is based least of all on quantitative research. But the validity and impact of that contribution have been no less influential as a result. During the past three decades the feminist movement has been primarily responsible for the establishment of protective centres for battered women (once referred to as 'battered wives units'), rape victims and children who have been sexually abused by their parents or relatives (rape and incest centres). Feminists have also been instrumental in counselling the victims, providing group and individual therapy, and in offering alternatives to a return to the source of their abuse. In these centres women have felt safe enough to recall, in graphic detail, the experiences of multiple abuse to which they have been subjected. What have also emerged, however, are harrowing accounts of the sexual abuse they endured in their childhood. These accounts, frequently published in feminist and social work journals, are more profound, informative and relevant than any research or opinion poll findings. They are a lot more credible too, in conveying the cunning and strategy of abusers, and in their analysis of the abuser's character and motivation.

Analysis

The feminist analysis of child sexual abuse is dominated by the concept of 'power' (Coveney *et al.* 1984; Hadley 1987; Herman and Hirschman 1977; MacLeod and Saraga 1987). This concept derives from a more fundamental philosophical position on male–female relationships generally, where the central tenet asserts that male sexuality is an instrument of male control over women. Jeffries (1984: 14) suggests: 'in its extreme form the construction of male sexuality and its relationships to power is revealed by the selection of children as (sexual) partners'.

The conviction that sexual abuse of children is an abuse of power over those children is not shared by feminists alone. Sgroi (1982a: 9) writes: 'Authority and power enable the perpetrator, implicitly or directly, to coerce the child into sexual compliance.' She later adds: 'abuse of power tends to be a way of life and a dominant aspect of family interaction in incestuous families' (p. 118). The American National Centre on Child Abuse And Neglect actually defines child sexual abuse in terms of an abuse of power: 'contacts or interactions between a child and an adult when the child is being used for the sexual stimulation of the perpetrator or another person when the perpetrator is *in a position of power or control over the victim*' (1978: 42).

There are many critics of the feminists' preoccupation with male power in their analysis of the causes of child sexual abuse (Dale 1987; Dale *et al.*, 1986a; Ennew 1986; Pierce 1987). They rightly point out that feminists ignore the considerable number of boys who are sexually abused, and that they are reluctant to 'acknowledge the passive role of women' in many child sexual-abuse cases (Dale 1987). Ennew (1986) is particularly critical of the feminist view which does not differentiate between women's rights and the rights of children, and which assumes 'the oppression of women and children to be identical in cause and manifestation' (p. 57). There may be some justification in these criticisms, but they do not invalidate the central stand of feminists on child sexual abuse being fundamentally an abuse of power. In my own experiences, i.e. twelve years of generic social work, and the last two years specializing in child abuse and child sexual abuse in an inner-city area, the abuse of power by the perpetrator has been one of the most conspicuous features of child sexual-abuse cases.

Feminist history and literature

Feminists have not always been preoccupied with such notions as the 'social construction of male sexuality' (Jackson 1984). In the latter half of the nineteenth century they had far more basic preoccupations: they wanted the vote, the repeal of the Contagious Diseases Acts, the raising, for girls, of the age of consent to sexual intercourse to sixteen. The struggles behind these and other goals are particularly relevant to the current debates on child sexual abuse. Take for example, their campaigns against the Contagious Diseases Acts. These acts enabled the authorities to compel prostitutes to be medically examined, and, if found to have any sexually transmitted disease, to be detained for treatment. Naturally feminists were in the vanguard of opposition, rightly protesting that the male customers of prostitutes were equally – if not more so – likely to spread such disease. The simple, crude and corrupt conviction behind the acts, however, was that *women were responsible*. (Anyone who believes that this is an historical irrelevancy should reflect on the government's recent decision to have all pregnant women tested for AIDS.)

In addition to political and social campaigning, there is a branch of feminist literature in this early period which is rich in its comment upon the sexual abuse of women generally. In the present reawakening about the consequences of the sexual liberation of the sixties, and the increasingly frantic efforts by governments to stem the inexorable spread of AIDS, feminists may justifiably proclaim that many of their earliest predecessors could have predicted the present crisis, more importantly that the 'cure' they would have recommended is most likely to be the one that will be universally adopted. In stark contrast to that branch of feminism which wholly supported the sixties' sexual liberation, some prominent feminists in this earlier period preached a gospel of sexual restraint more akin to that of a papal encyclical! Ethelmer (1897) and Swiney (1907), for example, argued that the only effective remedy for sexual abuse of any kind was for sexual intercourse to take place strictly for the purposes of procreation. Swiney was particularly incensed by the presumably widespread male insistence on sexual gratification when the woman was already pregnant: 'there is no greater shame attached to a man' (p. 33). Hamilton (1909) and Pankhurst (1913) later argued that frequent sexual intercourse was neither necessary nor desirable for women, indeed, was positively harmful. Experimentation in artificial birth control was frowned upon, the only effective control in their opinion that of abstinence. Such views would have been laughed at in the sixties, no less than by feminists themselves. Today, there is widespread respect for them, with feminists realizing better than most that the so-called sexual liberation they so enthusiastically greeted in the sixties was an illusion, indeed probably a major contribution to the increase in the sexual abuse of women generally (Jackson 1984). It seems that there were fewer illusions amongst pioneering feminists, and perhaps the last word on their contribution should be made by Millicent Fawcett, a prominent campaigner against sexual exploitation and the laws which sustained it:

> And when a father towards a child, a guardian towards a ward, a master towards a servant, is guilty of using the position of authority the law gives him, to induce the child or servant to commit immoral actions, the offence ought to be recognized and punished as having a special degree of gravity.
>
> (1892: 17)

Current feminist policy and practices

Current feminist policy and practice are naturally constructed around extensive experience in working with women victims of sexual abuse generally. The protective and therapeutic centres for abused women, incest victims and sexually abused children remain crucially important resources for victim, volunteers and professional agencies alike. The feminist focus has nevertheless widened considerably (Boushel and Noakes 1988). Wood-croft (1988) acknowledges 'the guilt and anguish felt by the child if a father is arrested by the police and eventually sent to prison' (p. 126). In what must be regarded as a radical departure from the feminist tradition of having no sympathy for perpetrators, she argues for new provision within the existing legal system that would enable a perpetrator to 'undergo therapy or treatment if for example, he wishes to have access to the child' (p. 123). Perhaps the most striking feature in this widening focus is the change of attitude towards the police (in the light of the way many women victims have been treated by the police); the earliest contact, close co-operation and mutual respect between the social worker and the police throughout the whole process of disclosure and investigation are now seen as paramount. Islington Social Services has recently adopted a feminist policy and response embracing all of these changes. It clearly states the need for: 'a clear theoretical perspective on abuse and abusers'; 'an awareness that reception into care . . . can be extremely painful and destructive'; 'working closely with the police in child sexual abuse cases', and, it suggests, that rehabilitation may actually be contemplated, provided that it is 'developed with a great deal of caution and includes safeguards for the child' (Boushel and Noakes 1988: 151–4).

It remains to be seen how a distinctly feminist practice, with details of technique, skill and strategy for each phase of intervention, evolves. But the experiences, literature and philosophy of feminism, in a hundred years of commitment to the eradication of child sexual abuse, will ensure that the feminist contribution is always a formidable one.

The family-therapy perspective

Family therapists' interest in child sexual abuse is a comparatively new development. Their analysis of the causes of such abuse within the family is not dissimilar to their analysis of family dysfunction generally. (The family-therapist perspective is often referred to as the 'family dysfunctional model'.) Family therapy has many theories of family function and dysfunction. One of the most prominent is systems theory, upon which family therapists have developed their analysis and treatment of child sexual abuse. (For a detailed explanation of family systems theory, see Walrond-Skinner 1976 and O'Hagan 1986a.) At the core of systems theory's explanation is the belief that sexual abuse plays a vital role in maintaining some kind of equilibrium, that each family member has a vested interest in sustaining the abuse, and that, if the abuse was suddenly terminated (by the removal of the child, for example), the family is likely to be plunged into crisis. Consequently 'possessiveness, secrecy and guilt can pervade the family life' in order to maintain this 'solution' of abuse, 'and the solution becomes a problem in its own right' (Mrazek and Mrazek 1981).

Certain patterns of relationships and characteristics of individuals in incestuous families have been observed by numerous family therapists. Furniss (1983: 265) for example, observes:

a sexually frustrated but demanding father, who is emotionally immature and dependent upon his wife as a mother figure; a sexually rejecting mother who is either compulsively caring for her husband or needs him due to her own emotional deprivation; and a daughter who has no trusting emotional relationship with her mother which could protect her from the incest.

Mrazek and Mrazek (1981) explain the origins of what systems family therapists would regard as a typical child sexual-abusing situation in a family as follows: The father is becoming impotent and fears that his wife will leave him. He sexually approaches his nine-year-old daughter. She has an idealized image of her father and needs his attention and approval for her own image to be maintained. Her positive responses to dad reassure him about his masculinity. Mother then may well be spared having to meet her husband's sexual needs. The family then begin to share a myth that sexuality between father and daughter is an acceptable part of a family's life together. Given this explanation, there can be only one strategy of intervention: 'Stopping the sexual abuse is not enough. The underlying family dynamics must be addressed' (p. 172).

In both of these and in many other examples the role of the mother is seen as crucial. The implication is clear and is often explicitly declared: mother's role is a powerful contributory factor in the origin and maintenance of the abuse. Her motivation is explained by terms like 'collusion', 'passivity', 'a willing deception' and an overwhelming need to 'protect the perpetrator'. There is no empirical basis for this explanation, merely an impression by writers and practitioners – mostly male – that mothers wittingly or unwittingly contribute to the abuse. Kempe and Kempe (1978: 66) go so far as to state: 'we have simply not seen an innocent mother in long-standing incest, although the mother escapes the punishment that her husband is likely to suffer'. Similarly, when the abuse has been exposed, the reactions of these 'guilty' mothers are perceived in the worst possible way:

> Either the mother colludes with the father to expel the daughter as the source of moral evil in the family, or the mother colludes with the daughter against the father who is seen as the only guilty party.
>
> (Furniss 1983: 274)

This alleged 'collusion' of mothers is not confined to the sexual abuse of daughters. Minuchin and Fishman (1981: 101) describes an approach to the case of a fifteen-year-old son being sexually abused by his father:

> The therapist . . . is especially concerned with avoiding a linear allocation of blame. The father has been abusing his child, but the wife has clearly been colluding, and by now the boy is a willing participant in the total process. The therapist also surmises that the husband's abuse of his son is at least partially an expression of problems between the man and his wife.

Family-therapy treatment programme

This perspective clearly indicates the direction and goal of the family therapist's intervention. Existing relationships, boundaries and structures within the family have got to be exposed and gradually replaced by something entirely different. Father must admit and accept responsibility for the abuse, but mother must also accept that she has failed to protect and has actually contributed to it. Far greater emphasis is placed upon 'normalizing' the relationship between mother and daughter than on punishing or rehabilitating the father. Family therapists are cautioned about the enormous resistance that abusing families – including the victim – will muster when treatment is being attempted (again, not unlike the resistance demonstrated by dysfunctional families generally (Minuchin 1974)). Various techniques and strategies are available for surmounting such resistance (Dale *et al.* 1986a and b; Furniss 1983; Minuchin and Fishman 1981). They are identical to the techniques and strategies which were devised in family-therapy practice long before family therapists began focusing on child sexual abuse.

Criticisms of the family-therapy perspective

There has been increasing criticism of some of the focal tenets in the family-therapy perspective. Bowlby (1988), one of the founder members of the family-therapy movement, criticizes the notions of 'convenience' and 'advantage': 'I don't see the child's behaviour as in any way advantageous'. He believes there is no consistency in the matter of who does or does not benefit from symptomatology. 'I can think of many families where maternal grandmother is benefiting and the other members of the system, mother, father, child, are all disadvantaged' (p. 6).

The belief that mother colludes in the abuse has provoked much criticism by feminists (MacLeod and Saraga 1987, 1988a and b). This is hardly surprising, as it is obvious from the typical quotations in family-therapy literature given above that the authors have not been over aware of the implications of what they write, nor of the impact on their readers as a whole. I have consistently advocated the use of family therapy based upon systems theory in many spheres of social-work practice, particularly for family crisis intervention (O'Hagan 1980, 1986a). But it is the very success of family therapy which has convinced its proponents that its theories, strategies, skills and techniques can simply be applied to *all* spheres of practice. Some of the thinking and analyses of family-therapy theories cannot and should not be so easily applied to child sexual abuse, if only because they are as insulting to the victim as they are inaccurate in diagnosis. The major dangers in the family-therapy perspective are, first, its enormous scapegoating potential, i.e. the abused child, the 'colluding' mother; and, second, as a consequence of the first, its unwitting contribution to a substantial segment of the general public who find it easy and convenient to believe that the mother of a sexually abused child must have played some part in the abuse. As the pitiful Myra Hindley has painfully discovered, there is no greater nor unforgivable crime in the minds of that public than that of a woman who colludes in the sexual abuse of a child by her male partner. There are at last clear indications that the family therapists have awakened to these dangers, and that terms like 'collusion' and 'the abuse is only a symptom of . . .' are less central and more seldom used in the explanation of the family-therapy perspective (Bentovim 1987, 1988).

The humanist perspective

The humanist perspective of child sexual abuse evolved mainly from the work of Henry Giarretto, and from the Child Sexual Abuse Treatment Programme (CSATP) he devised in the early seventies, in Santa Clara, California (Giarretto 1978, 1981). The term 'humanistic', which Giarretto uses liberally in his writings, has not been defined but is easily understood as a reactive campaign on his part to what he perceived as society's and the law's purely punitive responses to child sexual abuse. This perspective is unique nonetheless as, unlike the feminist and family-therapy perspectives, it does not recognize any single person or relationship or societal or cultural influence as the dominant or most common contributory factor in sexually abusive families. Even less so does it attribute blame, innocence or guilt.

There are two revolutionary aspects of the CSATP; first, it seeks to generate the 'humanistic, community-rooted climate, in which sexually abused children, perpetrators, and other family members, are supported during the crisis period' (Giarretto 1981: 180). Second, its success is based upon a shared conviction and commitment amongst key welfare, legal and penal agencies. Giarretto realized far sooner than most that the most punitive response to child sexual abuse was also the most damaging for the child victim. Rather than being preoccupied with finding the cause of the abuse, he was more interested in society's punitive response, and the analysis of that had to begin with himself. In a famous quote, Giarretto tells of his own revulsion on hearing the details of a particularly perverted abuse of a ten-year-old girl by her father. More revealing, however, is the revelation that his revulsion is triggered off by the same incestuous impulses within himself:

> I felt murderous . . . I forced myself to go into deep exploration of my unconscious for my own incestuous impulses . . . working through the incest-related garbage within me . . . I felt I could at least face my client.
>
> (Renvoize 1982: 191)

What may be implied here is that the orthodox and purely punitive response to child sexual abuse stems from our own unacknowledged fear of the potential for similar abuse within ourselves. Giarretto inspired numerous professionals and volunteers with these convictions. The recipients of the radical new service he was devising were not only inspired, but indebted too. Consequently many of the child victims, the abusing parents and the non-abusing parents eagerly responded to what became the central goals of CSATP; massive self-help amongst the abused, the abuser and all family members, community education, fund raising, and local and national advertising and publishing. The success of these initiatives achieved another more crucial goal, the removal of a crippling, terrifying fear associated with child sexual abuse, and often shared by victim and perpetrator alike, namely the fear of perpetual isolation, stigma and shame.

CSATP gave impetus to the American debates on child sexual abuse. Other perspectives began to emerge, advocating their own particular treatments. These were not invariably based upon the CSATP model; on the contrary, some are a reaction to it, rejecting all its ideals and practices. It is in the convictions about what constitutes the 'necessary' response to child sexual abuse by the police and the judiciary that these perspectives and their treatment models differ considerably. They are not wholly American in origin, but American practitioners and theorists can take credit for advancing each of them in terms of conceptualization and coherence. Again it should be stressed that, unlike the dominant British perspectives on child sexual abuse, which have evolved from (and have not advanced much further than) the political, ideological and systems/ psychoanalytical analyses of child sexual abuse, and which have formulated treatment programmes invariably confined to the victim – or, in very few instances, to the non-abusing family members – the American perspectives and their treatment programmes are far more preoccupied with embracing the crucially important agencies of police and judiciary in whatever course of action they are advocating. MacFarlane and Buckley (1982) have studied the models in detail, and it is upon their study that the following synopsis of the principal models is based.

Child sexual-abuse treatment programmes

The victim-advocacy model
This treatment model espouses the orthodox punitive response to child sexual abuse: it is a grave crime, deserving of severe penalties. The imposition of such penalties demonstrates society's abhorrence of the crime, and its recognition of the ordeal of the victim.

The improvement model
MacFarlane and Buckley define this model as 'embracing but humanizing the system' (p. 76). It is similar to the victim advocacy model in its central focus upon the child and in its encouragement of criminal prosecution. But it does not 'endorse prosecuting the criminal simply because it is a crime . . .' nor does it 'support incarceration of abusers in all cases . . .' (p. 77). The advocates of improvement seek to enlighten the police and the judiciary about the dynamics of child sexual abuse in order to gain more flexible and alternative responses that will encourage perpetrators to plead guilty.

The systems-modification model: creating systemic changes in legal intervention
This model is very much based upon Giarretto's CSATP. It seeks a major restructuring of legal procedures and processes. Its principal concern is to avoid the far greater damage perpetrated upon the victim by the traditional legal processes. It recognizes that imprisonment of the perpetrator invariably does little or nothing for the child, family or society. It advocates a massive involvement by the criminal justice system in the post-prosecutory and conviction phase, imposing and supervising treatment of the perpetrator and any therapy or treatment on offer to the whole family. It clearly delineates the functions of the juvenile and criminal courts in the service of the model, e.g. the criminal court is acknowledged as the primary vehicle for protecting the child (i.e. ordering the perpetrator to be removed from the home), while the juvenile court may be invoked if the non-abusing parent has ambivalent feelings towards the perpetrator or the child. Its guiding principle is that the goals of punishment and retribution should be replaced by the goal of rehabilitation.

The independent model
As its name implies, this model operates entirely upon the wishes and professional judgement of a limited number of professionals, e.g. psychiatrists, psychologists, medical personnel, irrespective of whatever other relevant agencies – particularly the police and the judiciary – may think or do about the abuse. The common view as to the origin and causes of child sexual abuse amongst these professionals is that it is 'an illness or family problem which requires specialized therapeutic resources'. The remedy has far less to do with how the magistrates or judges perceive matters than it has with counselling, self-help groups, sex therapy and educational techniques.

The system alternative model
This may be viewed as the more extreme form of the independent model. It rejects the involvement of law-enforcement agencies, the use of the terms 'offenders' and 'defendants' and adamantly proclaims that child sexual abuse is symptomatic of illness and/or dysfunctional behaviour patterns within the whole family which require therapeutic intervention. Its opposition to the involvement of either the juvenile or criminal courts is philosophically based: a conviction that court orders and legal coercion of any kind are merely 'artificial mechanisms for commanding clients' physical presence at therapy sessions' (p. 82). This is not the way to generate a genuine motivational force towards therapy, and the advocates of this model believe that the so-called radical departures from the punitive approaches to child sexual abuse, in which the courts 'demand' and 'order' an offender to behave in a certain way, is 'antithetical to the concept of psychotherapeutic treatment' (p. 82).

The Godfather offer

This is basically an offer to the perpetrator to avoid criminal prosecution and harsh penalties in exchange for his admission of guilt and his willingness to accept treatment. Where criminal prosecution is inevitable, avoidance of a harsh sentence may be offered in return for a guilty plea. The objectives behind the Godfather technique are both pragmatic and opportunistic, serving not just the child's interests (he/she will not have to testify, nor have to feel guilty when the perpetrator's sentence is deferred or cancelled) but also serving the criminal-justice system (saving the expense and time of litigation), the treatment providers and programme (the abuser is not likely to drop out of treatment because of the continuing threat of punishment or prosecution), other family members (who will have the opportunity to avoid the expense and stigma of a public trial, and to receive therapy to work through dysfunctional behaviour, even if separation is required). These objectives are also, of course, pursued in the more conceptualized and more philosophically identifiable programmes above, but it is precisely the lack of a fundamental philosophical base which differentiates the Godfather technique. Indeed, the morality of it may be questionable to some, as the major thrust is geared towards gaining a confession from the perpetrator. Unless there are clear instructions and criteria for so doing, there must be the very real danger of gaining that confession through legally and morally unacceptable means.

The American way?

For over fifty years various professional welfare groups in Britain have been encouraged and inspired by American literature, theory and practice in their own respective fields. The American way was always seen as the more progressive and enlightened way. The benefit of reviewing (albeit so briefly) the above perspectives and treatment programmes is a realization that American professionals themselves, rightly so, do not hold the same view. They are far more aware of the enormous diversity of American perspectives and treatments, some of them diametrically opposed and none of them universally accepted or popular. I was reminded of this fact a few years ago when I worked in California for a brief period. I had gone there believing that the American way of responding to child abuse generally was more advanced than our own – particularly the Californian way! I worked in a residential establishment for homeless families and destitutes, mostly of Hispanic origin. There was an Indian mother there, with two small children, and a loud-mouthed, massively built, most obnoxious cohabitee, who treated her and the children abominably. Someone reported this mother to the state-sponsored Child Protection Agency, alleging that she was abusing and neglecting the children. A social worker from the agency arrived, mid-morning. The cohabitee had left. Lots of residents and staff stood around, but many began drifting away, when the social worker's intention became clear. He didn't bother seeking any privacy for his visit. He simply confronted her with the allegation and then proceeded to interrogate her. He made numerous insulting references to the children's unkempt appearance. His voice got louder and more aggressive. He left her, gesticulating his finger with a warning that, if he had to call again, he'd remove the children from her.

It would be naïve and grossly prejudicial to regard this social worker's response as 'the American way'; but so too would it be naïve in the extreme to believe that Giarretto has converted the nation to his particular beliefs about child sexual abuse, and that we in Britain can easily follow suit. There is, however, a common factor underlying these two examples. The practices of Giarretto and that social worker are only possible because they satisfy the views and feelings of significant persons in their own organizations and/or communities. In the case of the former, great industry, conviction and determination were needed to educate, lead and convince the community about the merits of a radically different *all-embracing* treatment programme for child sexual abuse. In the case of the latter, mutual gut instincts on baby batterers sufficed for an *all-embracing* practice as brutal and ineffective as it is short sighted. Are there any lessons here for British front-line staff and their respective managements trying to respond effectively to child sexual abuse?

Summary and conclusions

It is now time to be more discriminating in our perceptions of the abundant training and literature on child sexual abuse. Paradoxes, confusions and uncertainties have been revealed, indicative of a lack of clear purpose and relevancy. The fundamental questions to ask are: what form does the literature and training take? does it describe the personally recorded experiences of victims? does it seek to present, explain, criticize or advocate particular perspectives on child sexual abuse? does it provide research and statistical findings? does it describe or recommend specific sets of procedures? does it construct or review treatment programmes? The second question is crucial: how relevant are each of these forms and their contents to the specific child sexual-abuse tasks encountered in our own unique working context? Three of the most prominent perspectives on child sexual abuse have been reviewed. The experiences, philosophy, literature and history of the feminist movement give its perspective a dimension and authority that have not as yet been recognized or appreciated. The humanist perspective has led to the establishment of comprehensive treatment programmes, embracing the efforts of professionals, volunteers, victims and families, and the police and judiciary. The long-established criminalization of child sexual abuse and the public's revulsion to it give the police and the judiciary a crucial role in the implementation of any treatment programme, be it purely punitive or radically humane. A review of numerous treatment programmes has revealed an enormous diversity in philosophy and practice, but the common factor and conclusion can only be that these diversities mirror those that exist in the surrounding communities and key agencies. An awareness and influence within the varying political and legal contexts of child sexual-abuse incidence is therefore of fundamental importance; particularly so, if any attempt is being made to provide an alternative to the traditional strictly punitive, child-centred, family-ignored responses, now so discredited.

4
Ethical considerations in child sexual-abuse work

Introduction

The subject of ethics has been largely ignored in child sexual-abuse literature. Writers and professionals have not been too concerned about this for the convincing reason that they already operate within the strict ethical principles of well-established professional ethical codes. This chapter will ask why has there been so much discrepancy and even contradiction in professionals' 'ethical' perceptions and practices in child sexual-abuse work. Some answers will be suggested. A brief historical view of ethical considerations will follow, highlighting significant shifts in the perceptions of clients and their problems, and the arrival of the concepts of 'rescue' and 'protection' as the dominant ethical goals in child sexual-abuse work. These terms and others similar have often been exploited; quoted from ethical codes and used as mere catchphrases and platitudes, behind which professionals can take refuge from the complexities and challenges of their responsibilities. 'The rights of the parents versus the rights of the child' is another generality similarly misused. A precise meaning of this term will be sought, through differentiating between parental circumstances in child sexual-abuse cases. A key differentiation is that between parents who participate in the abuse in some way and those who don't. The 'rights of the child' concept has to be examined in the broadest sense of the overall contribution the family and parents are making towards the child's development. Despite the misuse of these ethically loaded terms, the established professional codes of ethics still offer sound, explicit, ethical principles and guidelines. The most significant of these revolve around the issues of the accumulation of knowledge, multi-disciplinary co-operation and agency resources. Each of these will be explored.

Finally ethical considerations will be pursued through an actual case. It will be seen that there are ethical obligations in child sexual-abuse work which are not usually acknowledged in other spheres of work, obligations to the referrer, for example. The ethical importance of the 'knowledge base' and multi-disciplinary co-operation will be demonstrated, and the chapter will conclude by outlining the immensely pragmatic advantages to the management of cases, when professionals adhere to ethical principles.

Child sexual abuse: the ethical challenge

Many writers on the topic of child sexual abuse, and the practitioners who read their works, can be excused for a scant regard to the question of ethics. The welfare professions are steeped in ethics; their members, i.e. doctors, psychiatrists, paediatricians, health visitors, nurses and social workers, continually refer to 'the ethics of their profession', meaning a system of values long ago established by their predecessors, and relied upon daily as the guarantor that their actions are always in the interests of all their clients. Disasters may occur, new client groups may emerge, different policies may be called for; but the ethical code upon which policies are formulated remains the same; its tenets are perceived as permanently sound and good, and they ring forth in clear unambiguous tones; they are not subject to change.

This may be so in respect of how professions have been functioning in the past. But the contradictions, chaos and varying degrees of conflict and helplessness which all professionals have recently experienced and observed amongst themselves in their response to child sexual abuse suggests that, whatever ethical code (if any) has been determining professional practice, it has been a seriously deficient one. The fact is that child sexual abuse is a virtually limitless field in terms of the number of its complex component parts, and in terms of the number of ethical issues arising out of each of those component parts. Writers are only beginning to grapple with the sheer dimensions of child sexual abuse; they can hardly have been expected at this early stage to have dwelt upon its ethical complexities. Even less so those professionals, particularly social workers, who have been overwhelmed by the practical and emotional demands it has made upon them. Neither they nor their managers have had time to explore the relevance or adequacy of existing ethical codes, let alone had time to ponder what might have to be put in their place. The consequence has been that many of the professional responses to child sexual-abuse referrals, and the investigations and interventions which have followed, have been without ethical scrutiny. Ironically many senior social-work personnel claimed during the Cleveland inquiry that they were guided in their actions by their own profession's ethical code. Given the consequences, it is necessary to enquire about the relevance of such a code to the ethical challenges which child sexual-abuse work poses.

Ethics: a brief historical perspective

On the face of it, there should be no 'ethical' complications in child sexual-abuse work: innocent children are being harmed by adults from whom they cannot escape, and those children have got to be rescued. This simple fact is very similar to the core idea of the ethical principles of social work in its earliest years: the client was a victim, unfairly treated by all and sundry, and needing rescue and protection provided by the social worker. Thus the 'casework' domination of social work (Biestik 1961; Heywood 1964; Perlman 1957); the one-to-one relationship between worker and a 'weak, oppressed client', the social worker's commitment towards upholding the dignity of her client, and the client's right to self-determination. This ethical theme continued until the early seventies, when the wider focus of the family therapists was being accepted as more pragmatically and ethically realistic. The client was not so oppressed and was only a constituent part of a much larger social group, each of whose members had rights and welfare that were every bit as important as those of the originally diagnosed client. O'Hagan (1986a) went much further and demonstrated that some 'clients' can be murderous (towards social workers and other professionals), mentally ill, perverted, cruel, manipulative and/or destructive to those all around them. He argued that the 'armchair-casework morality' in the social-work literature of the sixties was irrelevant in training social workers to cope when faced with powerful, dangerous and manipulative clients, particularly in crisis situations (e.g. crisis of the mentally ill or violent crises between adolescent stepchildren and stepparents). This made it 'ethically' imperative for workers who were going to find themselves in these situations to acquire skills and techniques that would give them power, authority and control, to be exercised for the safety of client, family and worker alike.

The literature on child sexual abuse has reverted in a sense to the scenario projected in the sixties, that of the defenceless and innocent client (now the sexually abused child) at the mercy of an all powerful, unscrupulous, (usually male) adult, from whom he or she must be rescued and supported by the professional. Thus the emphasis upon the 'ethical' obligation to rescue and protect. Yet Lamb's (1986) article on the treatment of sexually abused children criticizes this attitude. She argues that professionals who persistently instil in the minds of child victims the notion that they were totally innocent, helpless and powerless, whilst they were being abused, may succeed more in reinforcing and perpetuating that sense of helplessness in the child's later life. She says: 'Saying "it's not your fault" is not helpful because it does not address the sense of power and control that children who have experienced sexual abuse often feel . . .' (p. 305). This is a most unusual theme in the literature and would be strongly resented by feminists. (Yet it is echoed very powerfully in a feminist's novel, *Union Street* (Barker 1982), in which the eleven-year-old Kelly, raped in the back streets of her own home town, acquires a power and influence over her attacker that reduces him to tears.) Lamb suggests that professionals should emphasize to the victim what she claims they already know (even very young children), that the abuse situation is one containing a number of choices for the child: 'Teaching children that some of their choices showed poor judgement is not to label them as "bad", but to point out that children have merely not yet learned enough about the world to make the best choice in certain situations' (p. 306). Be that as it may, Lamb is saying nothing different from any other writer on the matter of the perpetrators' criminality and immorality, for which they remain wholly accountable. The ethics governing the professionals' response to such a situation are quite straightforward; the paramount duty – the ethical obligation, backed by law, public morality and common decency – is to put a stop to that abuse.

Catchphrases and platitudes in the guise of ethics

That may well be so, but numerous problems arise, for social workers in particular. First, social workers have never been in the business of merely rescuing clients as an end in itself; they rightly believe that their obligations extend well beyond rescue and are much more complicated. Second (as we have clearly seen in the first chapter), even though many innocent defenceless children are being abused by powerful adults, there is a context surrounding that abuse which, even if social workers were so inclined, makes it impossible merely to rescue their client. Rescuing a sexually abused child necessitates an intervention which will have a massive impact upon that context, for good or ill; it is likely to have the greater impact upon the child itself. Thirdly, 'rescuing' is universally perceived as synonymous with 'the welfare of the child'. But whilst there is no difficulty in explaining what rescuing means, there are few professionals in the field of child sexual abuse who would feel confident in giving the definitive explanation of the child's welfare. As Warnock (1987: 19) has written about her experiences in chairing the 1982 Committee of Inquiry into human fertilization:

> Although there is a verbal harmony between the many voices, all of them intoning the solemn words 'the good of the child', there is a good deal less agreement about what the good of the child might actually be.

This lies at the heart of the ethical dilemmas of child sexual-abuse work. Social workers and many other professionals have lost sight of it in a confusion between 'the good of the child' and 'the good of the professional', the latter invariably meaning to be able to return to one's home and family at night, knowing that one had at least put a stop to the awful sexual abuse of an innocent child. As many social workers have later found out, however, that is not necessarily serving 'the good of the child'.

Ethics is supposed to be a system of values which guarantee that professionals' attitudes and behaviour towards their clients always serve the interests and welfare of those clients. But the nature of child sexual-abuse work is such that it compels social workers to have to face many different persons besides one individual client, to be facing them, and interacting with them, and making decisions about them at numerous and different times. In each of these countless experiences, any perception of the welfare of the child is likely to undergo significant change; for example, the first encounter with the abused child Sarah convinced the social worker that it was in Sarah's interest to be 'protected' from the sexual abuse which was allegedly taking place; but as the social worker encountered more individuals and situations, learnt more about the family and social context of the abuse and became aware of very serious shortcomings in the department's resources and responses, that perception drastically altered.

'Protection' is probably the most common platitude. It has been used (abused) in defence of a multitude of unethical practices. Ironically it is of itself a wholly ethical and laudable objective but, when pursued in practice on behalf of a child, the ethical quality of action will be determined by the worker's interactions with the child's family and social context, and by the means by which the protection is implemented. There is not much protection being offered to a child by a worker whose intervention turns the parents against that child; there is even less protection being offered in suddenly 'rescuing' a child and placing her with ill-prepared foster parents who do not know how to cope with sexually abused children.

The continuous harping on about 'protection', 'the interests of the child', 'the child's welfare' and 'the child comes first', etc., totally ignores the wider social and family contexts of the child and any legitimate enquiry about the quality of resources the department has at its disposal. Such catchphrases and platitudes are, of course, direct quotes from the ethical codes of professionals and child-welfare institutions. We can be certain that these phrases were adopted and were useful long before child sexual abuse was acknowledged as a problem. No one can question the sincerity or morality behind them, but as a framework for realistic child sexual-abuse policy-making, and the provision of detailed procedures and guidelines for front-line staff having to cope with the situation, they are misleading and unhelpful.

The rights of the parents versus the rights of the child

This rather more imposing phrase is nevertheless another sweeping generalization to emerge from ethical considerations. It is misused in the opposite sense to the way that platitudes are misused. The latter sound so all important and decisive as to justify any action on their behalf (for example, 'protection' justifies the drastic action of removal); the former is the least decisive and merely narrows all the complexities of a case into a paralysis-inducing, unresolvable conflict. Like many other phrases, however, it is conveniently applied to *all* child sexual-abuse cases.

If parents do not know their children are being abused, do not contribute to the abuse in any way and are shocked and angry in finding out, thus taking appropriate protective measures, their parental rights are not open to question. If parents on the other hand do actually abuse or facilitate the abuse in some way, then their rights are very much a matter for critical scrutiny and are secondary to the rights of the child. Between these two extremes, there are myriads of cases of varying degrees of innocence and non-involvement on the part of parents, and of responsibility and participation. But in order to justify any diminution of parental rights, a detailed assessment of the overall contribution they make to the child's general welfare has to be made, with particular attention to how the child might perceive and 'feel' that contribution and the prospect of being denied it in the interests of being 'rescued' and 'protected' from further abuse.

Ethics: the principal duties

Social-services policies are public policies. The public must understand and support them if they are to be implemented successfully. Before Cleveland, the public did support a vigorous implementation of the policy of rescuing children from child sexual abuse, and fully concurred with departmental spokespersons who explained that such policies naturally evolved from the overriding ethical pursuit of 'protecting the child'. The public is likely to have a more informed opinion now and are not likely to support the 'rescue' of children to the same extent again. There is, however, much more in professional ethical codes than mere platitudes. There are principal duties clearly stated; they cannot be misinterpreted or misused; they are unmistakably in the service of child, professional, organization and public alike. The three most significant are the pursuit of knowledge, the promotion of multi-disciplinary co-operation and agency resources.

Knowledge
All welfare professions are obliged to continually acquire knowledge and expertise upon which their ethical codes are formulated, modified, expanded and explained. Take, for example, the code of ethics of the British Association of Social Workers (BASW) (1988: paras 7 and 8). It says:

> Social work has developed methods of practice, which rely on a growing body of systematic knowledge and experience. The professional obligation must be acknowledged, not only to increase personal knowledge and skill, but also to contribute to the total body of professional knowledge.

Similar statements can be found in all professional codes of ethics. They are merely stating the obvious. Yet, on reflection, there is probably no period in the history of welfare institutions to compare with that of 1985–7 when so much feverish intervention and activity (in the field of child sexual abuse) was based upon so much ignorance about virtually every aspect of the problem and, above all, about the damaging impact of those interventions.

The only knowledge about which professionals could be certain, when they removed children, was that they were no longer being abused by a suspected perpetrator. Whatever else was happening to the children was a matter of debate. It is this fact of professional ignorance, rather than the damage perpetrated by (well-meaning) professionals, which justifies the claim that there was little ethical consideration of actions in Cleveland and elsewhere. Actions based upon ignorance, whether those actions are good or harmful, cannot be professional; even less so can they spring from any ethical code.

Multi-disciplinary co-operation

Another forgotten tenet in professional ethical codes is the duty to liaise, co-operate and work with other agencies which are also serving the client (this does not, however, apply to medical ethics which are dominated by the pursuit of confidentiality and privacy between patient and doctor). The acrimony revealed in the Cleveland report makes painful reading. There can be little doubt that the main protagonists, passionately believing that they were acting in the best interests of the clients, and believing equally passionately that others were not, were unaware of the unethical nature of that particular stance. Again, it is not the merits or demerits of the professional actions of one or the other in this situation which determines that the stance was unethical; it is the fact that in thought, word and deed, some strenuously and knowingly opposed each other in their service to the same clients. Whenever such a situation arises or, more pertinently, whenever it can be predicted, professionals have an obligation to inform and seek arbitration in their own respective managements. Comparatively, the lack of multi-disciplinary co-operation in Cleveland was an aberration, but the importance of such co-operation as an ethical factor and the professionals' obligation to promote it cannot be overemphasized.

Resources

'To diagnose [child sexual abuse] and not to provide service raises serious ethical questions' (Mrazek 1981: 15). If this statement was not given the significance it deserved when it was written, then the author can be assured that, after the child sexual-abuse crisis of 1987, professionals do acknowledge its meaning and its importance today. It is particularly meaningful to social workers, immersed as they often are in virtually every phase of child sexual-abuse work, and seeking many different types of resources during each phase, so that they can provide a quality of service that the sexually abused child requires. Resources are therefore very much an ethical issue, which is why the BASW code of ethics spells it out: 'They [the social worker] will acknowledge a responsibility to help clients to obtain all those services and rights to which they are entitled' (BASW, 1988: para. x). The corollary, of course, is that it is unethical for governments, local authorities, social-services departments and, not least, for individual professionals *not* to be striving towards the provision of necessary resources.

Ethics in practice

What are the circumstances of time, location and situation in child
sexual-abuse work which raise ethical questions and pose ethical challenges?
In what circumstances would a realistic, comprehensive ethical code be most
appreciated by front-line staff? The most effective way of exploring these
questions is by plotting one's ethical course through an imaginary case.

Mrs Jordan has three children, Siobhan, five; Margaret, three; and
Moira, eighteen months. She has recently remarried. Her husband, Mr
Jordan, is the father of the two younger children. Siobhan is the daughter of
her former marriage. The family have recently moved into a rather
dilapidated council estate. They quickly make friends. The couple are soon
able to get a neighbour to babysit for them. They have an occasional night
out. One evening, Siobhan confides in the neighbour and describes various
sexual abuses perpetrated against her by her stepfather. She describes
actions which quite clearly indicate fondling, oral masturbation, french
kissing, and simulated intercourse against her buttocks. Siobhan repeatedly
and decisively answers 'no' to the question: 'Does your mother know
anything about this?' The shocked neighbour does not know what to do. She
tells no one for a week and then, unable to keep quiet any longer, tells her
husband. They both decide to visit social services. They are both very
apprehensive about the outcome, as they dread that their actions might lead
to some kind of catastrophe.

Here is one of those typical cases in which the 'protection' of a very young
child is seen as the principal goal in a powerful ethical driving force. In
addition, the worker(s) will be merely carrying out the statutory task of
investigation and protection, if necessary. The problem in giving protection
such a high profile is that it can exclude the consideration of other aspects of
the abusing situation which are crucial in assessment. It can also cause the
worker to forget about the need for additional ethical considerations.

Ethical obligations to the referrer

Let us begin this ethical exploration at the referral phase. What, for
example, should the social workers' attitude and response be to two
responsible and caring neighbours who are, quite justifiably, frightened of
the consequences of their actions? (And in the light of Cleveland, who can
blame them?) It is very clear in this example that the social worker *does* have
some (ethical) responsibility for thanking, appreciating, reassuring and
supporting these neighbours, who have risked more to protect the child than
any professional is likely to risk. It would also seem obvious that, whilst the
social worker's primary responsibility is similarly to protect, she does have
an obligation to continually bear in mind the nature of the risk taken by the
neighbours, and, without complicating or magnifying the task of protection
in any way, to minimize that risk at every available opportunity. One

obvious task for the worker will be to 'sell' to a probably very angry mother of the child the reality that the neighbours have done her, as well as her sexually abused child, a great service in reporting the matter. There is, therefore, an ethical responsibility here which any ethical code should at least make implicit (for example, it could say something like: 'social workers must be sensitive to the public's feelings about and their perceptions of child sexual abuse generally; they should be particularly sensitive and supportive towards those members of the public who accept the risk of their contacting the department to express genuine concern about a particular child'. This ethical guideline should then be instrumental in instructing social-services managers when they are formulating policy on response to this particular kind of referral, and to the team leaders/supervisors, when they are negotiating the details of that response with their team members.

The 'ethical' pursuit of knowledge and planning

It is not so long ago that a referral like this would have triggered off an immediate and drastic intervention, leading to the very catastrophe which these good neighbours fear so much. The next ethical consideration, therefore, must be how to move towards the dominant ethical goal of protection without acting in a way which would make that catastrophe more likely. An ethical code will clearly point out, however, that much thinking and preparation have to be done before embarking upon any action. Numerous questions arise, reminding us that the pursuit of knowledge upon which action is based, is a central ethical tenet. These questions fall into two distinct groups. The first group arises out of the planning of strategy for this particular case. The second enquires about our knowledge base of the category to which this case belongs. We will look at the latter questions first:

1 How common is this particular case? Is the department responding to it as an isolated case, or is the response based upon any knowledge and familiarity with such cases in the past.
2 How vulnerable to sexual abuse is this child Siobhan, past and present? What more do we need to know about the family to be able to answer that question more accurately?
3 Assuming the abuse is occurring as described, how damaging is it to the child, short term and long term?
4 What are the characteristics in this home and family and parental relationships which have perhaps contributed to the risk of the child's being abused or have facilitated it?
5 What are the characteristics of the perpetrator, and what is it in his own childhood and upbringing (if anything) which has led him to abuse this child?
6 What aspects of this particular type of case pose the greatest challenge to social services?

7 What is the quality and quantity of resources needed by social services in making its contribution towards 'effectively' rescuing this child?

One point to stress immediately: such questions should not detract from the urgency of the case, nor can they be interpreted as an attempt to minimize the seriousness and criminality of what is being done to the child. In fact, these questions should not be necessary at all in response to any particular referral, because the assumption should be that front-line staff and their managers know the answers. The point that is being made here is that managers and social workers are ethically bound to know the answers or, if they don't, to be continuously striving to find out. It is obvious, in looking at any of these questions, that action based on not knowing the answers is likely to be qualitatively different from that based on knowing. It is this fact which warrants the importance attached to 'the accumulation of relevant knowledge' in any ethical code.

The questions above cover a wide area, but the answers are to be found in the study of three specific topics within child sexual abuse as a whole: research findings; the categorization of child sexual abuse; and perpetrators. These will be studied in more depth in the next three chapters.

The 'ethical' basis of strategy

There is a legal as well as an ethical obligation to inform the police about this referral. The consequences of that will vary enormously throughout the country. It could mean police on the doorstep minutes after they get the information. It could mean, on the other hand, the most careful joint planning and strategy. Obviously the latter is what must be implied as a crucial goal (if not explicitly stated) in an ethical code. Both agencies have an obligation to scrutinize their own and other agencies' records for any information about this family, particularly about the alleged perpetrator, before any joint meeting. Both must carefully consider how they advance on each stage of the investigative and intervention process and anticipate and prepare for all the consequences. The following are some ethical issues arising out of the more difficult challenges in this preparation:

1 If we assume that the child's evidence that mother doesn't know about the abuse is confirmed, what consideration is being given to ensuring mother's support of the child, her belief that such abuse has taken place, and her commitment towards ensuring that it will not take place in the future?
2 Where and when does the social worker/police officer intend interviewing the child, under what conditions, and with whom?
3 If the child repeats her allegations to the investigators, how will the workers recommend and facilitate a medical examination so that it will be accepted by mother?
4 What timing, location, atmosphere and process in a medical will cause least trauma for mother and daughter?

5 How should mother and child be prepared for the probability of the paediatrician's seeking to photograph signs of the abuse and, if mother objects, should she be supported?
6 If the medical examination is not conclusive, the alleged perpetrator denies it, the police feel that they have no basis for a prosecution, and the mother does not then know who to believe, is there an ethical basis for removing the child?
7 If the medical is inconclusive, and mother requested a second opinion, is there any ethical obligation to resist that or to facilitate it?
8 If the perpetrator admits abusing the child and is removed, what considerations are being given to ensuring that neither mother nor daughter will acquire feelings of guilt, to add to the feelings of devastation they may already have?
9 If a decision is taken to remove the child, how will this be carried out? If she is to be placed in a foster home, how experienced are the foster parents in caring for very young sexually abused children? How much access will be permitted between child and mother? where will it take place, and under what conditions? Will there be any access between child and stepfather if both request it?
10 If the child is removed, what are the ethical considerations, in addition to statutory obligations, which are most relevant in deciding whether or not the other children should be removed?

The pragmatism of ethical considerations

However difficult the above questions may be, they should also reassure workers that ethical considerations are eminently pragmatic. This is a point seldom appreciated in professional practice: that adhering to the principles of a sound ethical code will ensure the avoidance of many pitfalls, drastically reduce the number of obstacles in one's way, and prevent much needed allies and supporters from turning into sworn enemies. These regrettable developments occur every day in child sexual-abuse work. It is not because social workers or other professionals behave in a consciously unethical way. It is merely the consequence of the chaotic, undisciplined, pressure-laden, dangerous nature of that work. When this is coupled with an often ethically blind management, is it any wonder that 'ethical considerations' are seldom really considered? The less consideration given to ethics, the more professionals retreat to an ethically empty authoritarianism and cynicism. These are the principal ingredients of destruction and failure in child sexual-abuse work.

Summary and conclusions

It is understandable that ethics has not had a high profile in child sexual-abuse literature and training. Professionals and welfare bodies have had an abundance of ethical codes and guidelines, which, it was believed, sufficed in underpinning their professional practices. Considerable discrepancy in ethical perceptions and the practices stemming from them have, however, been exposed; terms and phrases denoting urgency and a strong ethical motivation have become mere catchphrases and platitudes, behind which unprofessional and unethical conduct can be concealed. The most common of these platitudes is 'the need to protect the child'. There are nevertheless principles of practice in existing codes which are fundamentally important in child sexual-abuse work. The three most significant emphasize the need for an accumulation of knowledge, multi-disciplinary co-operation and adequate agency resources. The ethical importance of each of these can be seen in a detailed scrutiny of the difficulties and challenges in any child sexual-abuse case; just as obvious are the practical advantages to be gained in all phases of investigation and intervention by giving sufficient time to ethical considerations, and adhering to ethical principles. The sexually abused child is the chief beneficiary.

5
The problem with research

Introduction

Researchers in the field of child sexual abuse invariably remark on the 'infancy' of their discipline, and on the need for much more research in many of the areas they regard as crucial (Berliner and Stevens 1982; Chandler 1982; Finkelhor 1986). This may well be the case, but it cannot conceal the fact that research literature on child sexual abuse has reached 'deluge' proportions, and that little or no attention has been given to the question of its value to practitioners. This chapter will approach that question from many different angles. It will critically review research literature and intermittently refer to the realities of practice. It will identify the principal areas of research and explore whether or not the findings can enable practitioners to cope more effectively when facing the major challenges in child sexual-abuse work. Is there any congruence or divergence between the principal areas of research and the major challenges in practice? What would researchers make of the experiences of Sarah and Elizabeth in the first chapter? of the tasks facing the professionals trying to 'protect' them, and of the ordeal of the parents suspected of abusing them? Are there any research studies or findings that might have influenced the professionals to act differently? The successful management of child sexual abuse can more easily be accomplished if it is conceptualized as a task that has clearly identifiable phases. Researchers and practitioners must therefore know which particular research is most applicable and helpful to which particular phase. Experienced cynical professionals who see no relevance in research studies are not the major obstacle to the recognition and appreciation of the value of research. Of far greater danger are those who persistently exploit research for their own purposes, by interpreting and applying the findings in a way that the researchers themselves would never justify. Such misuse was very common in the months preceding the crisis in Cleveland, when, for example, research statistics were quoted *ad infinitum* to demonstrate 'the high prevalence' of child sexual abuse, thus generating an uncritical anxiety that enabled professionals and their agencies throughout the country to respond in a manner which, we have all learnt, was most inappropriate.

Focus of research: prevalence

Child sexual-abuse researchers have been primarily concerned with establishing the *prevalence of*, and *the nature of* child sexual abuse. The question of prevalence has been particularly tantalizing for researchers. As one researcher in one particular location interprets his or her findings as an indication of high prevalence, so another researcher in another area may feel compelled to test out such findings. The resulting variations (Finkelhor 1986; Fontaine 1988) can only spur other researchers into more elaborate exploration, each one wanting to find the most accurate prevalence figure, based on the most methodologically sound research techniques. There is a snow-balling effect then, quite evident in the research literature, where one can see literally dozens of unrelated research attempts to establish what precisely the prevalence figure for general populations is. The more research there is, the more variation in the conclusions. Finkelhor (1986) suggests that these variations may stem from differences in definitions of child sexual abuse; different characteristics amongst different segments or races in the general population; different methodology. Another contributory factor, however, may be the motivation of the individuals upon whom the research is based; why some decide to disclose that they have been sexually abused in childhood, and some do not. Many reasons come to mind, but no one can be sure. Perhaps such motivation and all the other variables also need to be researched. As of yet, nobody seems to have asked why it should be so important that we know how many adults in the general population have been sexually abused in their childhood, or how such knowledge may enable professionals to respond more effectively to children who are being sexually abused today? The problem with this particular aspect of research is that it has to a large extent become an end in itself. Familiarity with the research and the articulate pronouncements on its findings have somehow acquired a status and authority for opinionating on all aspects of child sexual abuse; this has often been used as a means of intensifying the public's abhorrence of it, thereby distracting attention from the consequences of removing children from that abuse. Finkelhor (1986) cautions: 'The motivation behind prevalence studies can sometimes be more political than scientific . . .' (p. 52).

The nature of abuse: some problems in definition

Both in literature and in research efforts have been made to find a suitable definition of child sexual abuse. The range of abuses perpetrated against children is enormous, and the problems stemming from the abuse complex and demanding. A working definition is often seen therefore as the first intellectual and imaginative task in researching and in training for child sexual-abuse work. Schechter and Roberge's (1976: 60) definition is probably the most commonly used:

> the involvement of dependent, developmentally immature children and adolescents in (*sexual*) activities they do not truly comprehend, to which they are unable to give informed consent, or that violate the social taboos of family roles.

Two problems are immediately apparent here. First, many terms in this definition need definitions of their own, e.g. 'dependent', 'developmentally immature', 'do not truly comprehend', etc., and such terms may turn out to be crucial variables in assessing not just whether or not abuse has taken place, but also its seriousness and its effect. The second problem is precisely that it gives no clue to the varying degrees of seriousness and effect which, considering the enormous range of child sexual-abuse offences, is imperative.

Definition, therefore, as Finkelhor acknowledged, is a crucial factor in researching the prevalence of child sexual abuse. Surprisingly, the range of definitions or descriptions used by the researchers in approaching their study group varies almost as much as child sexual abuse itself. Finkelhor (1979) addressed his volunteers: 'We would like you to try to remember the sexual experiences you had while growing up. By "sexual", we mean . . . in fact, anything that might have seemed "sexual" to you.' A list of possible experiences then follows, including: 'An invitation or request to do something sexual. Another person showing his/her sex organs to you . . .' These two experiences, exhibitionism and verbal abuse, may indeed be unpleasant and even traumatic for the individuals involved. But the fact that there is no physical contact whatsoever between the individual and the potential perpetrator would cast doubt on either of them being termed child sexual abuse, and being used to substantially increase prevalence figures. It is significant that, although experiences like these have, without being specified, been included in child sexual-*abuse* statistics, the word 'abuse' seldom appears anywhere in researchers' questionnaires which have produced those statistics (Finkelhor 1986). Its inclusion may have inhibited many who volunteered to disclose such experiences.

Clearly much more rigour is necessary in the attempts to find a meaningful definition. It should embrace something far more than that in Burnam's (1985) research enquiry: have you ever been sexually assaulted in your childhood? and something less than Russell's (1983) which included every conceivable experience that fertile imaginations might perceive as child sexual abuse. It is no great problem if the 'right' definition cannot be found. Better to have no definition and to retain a healthy discriminatory approach to each recorded experience, than to seek a blanket definition applied to all experiences.

Children at risk of sexual abuse

At this point it is useful to stress some factors about child sexual-abuse research. First, it is nearly all American in origin. Second, it is directed mainly towards women. Third, as in the literature on child sexual abuse generally, it has been mostly concerned with incest. There have been very many more textbooks, personal testimonies and research projects on incest than on child sexual abuse (as the bibliographies will testify). The victims are usually adolescent girls, and the perpetrators more often fathers or stepfathers. It is important to bear these points in mind when examining the reasons why researchers have identified some groups of children to be more at risk than others.

Few research studies produce comprehensive and detailed profiles of the children who, when they reach adulthood, and are approached by researchers, disclose that they have been sexually abused. Researchers appear to have reached certain conclusions about high-risk children in the present general population on the basis of what adults remember about their 'sexual-abuse' experiences. It is reasonable to assume that one will remember the details of any sexual abuse in one's adolescence, particularly with a close relative, far more so than if one was sexually abused by a stranger before the age of five. Consequently, there is very little research evidence to indicate that children under five may be in a high-risk category. (My own experience in an inner-city area office tells me that they are.)

Finkelhor's (1986) analysis of designated high-risk children begins by making it clear that all research questionnaires were addressed to male as well as female respondents. But it seems that some of the important conclusions are based upon the experiences of girls alone. For example, Finkelhor draws attention to the researchers' nearly unanimous conclusions that *children* who have 'a poor relationship with their parents, particularly with their mother', are especially at risk. Yet on closer scrutiny one sees that the researchers reached this conclusion mainly, if not wholly, by interviewing *women*; to quote from Finkelhor: 'Landis (1956) was one of the first to observe that molested women reported a more distant relationship with their mothers'; 'Finkelhor (1984) found that those women at higher risk were the ones who said they were not close to their mothers, or who received little affection from their mothers or fathers'; 'Peters (1976) found that, for women, not being close to mother was the variable that was most predictive of sexual abuse' (Finkelhor 1986: 72–3). Similarly, with the conclusion that 'conflicting parents' and 'absent parents' are conspicuous features of child sexual abuse; the victims in the research are predominantly female, a factor later acknowledged by Finkelhor himself: 'All of these findings, on parental absence, poor relationships with parents, and conflict between parents – seem to point strongly towards the idea that sexually victimized *girls* have disturbances in their relationships with their parents' (p. 75).

There is more than a clear hint here that this whole research area, whether the researchers recognize it or not, is focusing entirely on father–daughter and/or stepfather–daughter incest. The conclusions may well be sound, if only to identify the parental situations conducive to high risk for adolescent girls. But what has to be regretted is that a whole package of factors identified in questioning women who were subjected to incestuous relationships with father figures, most likely during their adolescent years, have been adopted as risk criterion for numerous other age groups, and for boys, as well as girls.

Who are the respondents in researching high-risk categories?

It may have been noted that all the research aimed towards establishing the prevalence of child sexual abuse consists of retrospective studies, i.e. selecting groups of adults, many of whom are willing to acknowledge that they were sexually abused in childhood. One may well ask why no attempts have been made to establish prevalence on the basis of actual present-day incidence of abuse. The answer is that the child sexual abuse that does come to light is believed to be only a fraction of the amount that does actually take place. If the present-day reported incidence of abuse were analysed, it is likely that the poorer segments of society would be overrepresented in any findings, for the obvious reason that it is they who are most familiar and in most contact with numerous child-protective and law-enforcement agencies; consequently there is greater likelihood of sexual abuse in such families being exposed. This is another reason for preferring retrospective studies of the sexual abuse experienced by *cross sections* of the population.

But who are the people willing to respond to research questionnaires, face-to-face interviews, and telephone enquiries? Of one thing British social workers can be sure: such respondents are unlikely to be found in the areas they themselves frequent, i.e. the sprawling crime-ridden dilapidated inner-city slums and council estates, where fragmented families, poverty, overcrowding, and unemployment are the experiences of each day. However valid the claims that child sexual abuse is a classless phenomenon are, it is nevertheless a fact that the majority of sexual-abuse referrals social workers receive will be about children living in such areas. In concentrating upon the more economically viable and articulate populations, thereby avoiding the trap of labelling poverty-stricken children as the most vulnerable to sexual abuse, and correspondingly poverty-stricken parents as the most likely perpetrators, researchers have precluded discussion about the social and economic contributory factors in child sexual abuse. They have consequently failed to recognize what many social workers may regard as the most vulnerable groups of all; these are:

1 children with special needs, educational social and emotional, attending special schools, inarticulate and socially isolated, living in fragmented seriously deprived families.
2 Mentally handicapped children, living in similar circumstances.

Such children will never be consulted about whatever sexual abuse has been perpetrated against them. Researchers aim primarily at respondents who can at least speak. Then they choose a 'research group' that not only speaks but can articulate memory of events, often decades ago. In researching the prevalence of child sexual abuse, and in the national campaigns to prevent it, researchers and programmers have aimed for children and adults sophisticated enough to know what their research and efforts are about. For example, 'Childwatch', in October 1986, repeatedly asked children to come forward, tell the teacher, telephone the volunteers or authorities, and all this against a backdrop of a perfectly healthy, intelligent child of sufficient age, going into and coming out of the public telephone booth. This may have reassured the public, but it provoked some unease amongst professionals daily in touch with children too young or too physically, mentally, or emotionally handicapped to do what was being asked of them.

Why then might these two groups be more at risk than other children? Finkelhor (1984) provides the answer, in his conceptual framework for explaining the occurrence of child sexual abuse. Finkelhor believes that four preconditions need to be met before the abuse can occur.

1 A potential offender needs to have some motivation to abuse a child sexually.
2 The potential offender has to overcome internal inhibitions against acting on that motivation.
3 The potential offender has to overcome external impediments to committing sexual abuse.
4 The potential offender has to undermine or overcome a child's possible resistance to the sexual abuse.

There is much here that is open to interpretation. For example, a potential offender could have many motivations: sexual gratification, sexual curiosity, anger or hatred seeking sexual expression. Human handicap can be both a provocation and a curiosity for perpetrators, in addition to offering them the prospect of sexual gratification. The 'internal inhibitions' can be easily overcome by the perpetrator's rationalization of the planned abuse: 'that helpless handicapped person's life has been such a worthless life anyway, that abusing him or her won't make any difference'. In an age when governments, professionals, judges and juries are themselves rationalizing serious actions against handicapped persons (e.g. compulsory sterilization, so called 'mercy killing', etc.), it is hardly surprising that perpetrators could overcome their internal inhibitions in the same way. In number 3, 'external impediments' might simply mean getting caught or the risk of getting caught. There is much less risk of this happening when a child is too handicapped to point the accusing finger, or to describe the details of the abuse. As for number 4, these children will be the least resistant to the abuse, and the power imbalance between them and the perpetrator far greater. This powerlessness and inability to resist are powerful motivating factors in themselves.

The effects of child sexual abuse

Unlike prevalence research, heavily reliant upon retrospective studies, research on 'effects' relies on experiences of both past and present. One might think that researching present cases may be more straightforward and reliable; the reality is that 'effects' has more variables and pitfalls than any other aspect of research in child sexual abuse.

One cannot be surprised therefore by wildly varying research findings. Lukianowicz (1972) and Yorukoglu and Kemph (1966), for example, could find no ill effects in children who had incestuous relationships with a parent, whilst Chandler (1982) believes that incest is even worse than *violent* sexual abuse by a stranger. It is noticeable that the more recent the research, the more likely its findings will support the view that there are serious adverse effects of child sexual abuse. Chandler is, however, only one of a number of writers who begins her review of research on this matter by using findings on a specific type of sexual abuse, namely, rape. She makes reference to a number of writers (Burgess and Holmstrom 1974, 1979; Fox and Scherl 1972) who have produced evidence about the 'traumatizing effects of rape', but she fails to acknowledge that the respondents in these studies were women, not children. This is not to suggest that children do not suffer to the same extent as women (researchers and public alike should not need research findings to realize the enormity of the crime of rape, and the probability of very serious effects, irrespective of whether it is perpetrated against male, female, child or adult), but it might once again indicate how feelings about sexual abuse generally may blunt one's discriminatory approach to a specific aspect of the problem. There is probably as much 'feeling' about effects as there are variables, and writing and research on the matter has got to be looked at with caution.

Initial effects
Effects may be initial or long term. Initial effects have been reported by the parents of children and observed and charted by those who treat them. Tufts (1984) is one of the most comprehensive studies, repeatedly referred to in Finkelhor's review of research. It is based upon numerous educational and psychological tests of a number large enough to enable researchers to monitor different categories of effects in different age categories of children.

It found the seven-to-thirteen age group particularly vulnerable to serious initial effects (not a very discriminating age range in itself). Over 40 per cent of this group had the highest recorded levels of psychopathology, i.e. they were seriously disturbed. They were disturbed in terms of their overt behaviour, fear and levels of hostility. De Francis (1969) found 55 per cent of sexually abused children exhibiting serious behavioural disturbances, such as actual defiance and disruptive behaviour within the family. 'Fear' was the most common single consequence of the abuse in both of these studies: 45 per cent of the seven-to-thirteen age group in Tufts, and 83 per cent in De Francis.

The sleeping and eating difficulties which social workers have increasingly observed in sexually abused children are well supported by research findings. Peters (1976) found that 31 per cent of a group of children sexually abused within their families had sleep problems, and 20 per cent had difficulties in eating. Kaufman, Peck and Tagiuri (1954) support the former (i.e. sleep problems) and Burgess, Groth and McCauseland (1981) support the latter (eating difficulties).

Tufts (1984) concluded that 27 per cent of the four-to-six-year-olds and 36 per cent of seven-to-thirteen-year-olds demonstrated highly sexualized behaviour, e.g. openly 'sexual' advances towards adults, frequent masturbation, excessive sexual curiosity and frequent exposure of the genitals. The sense of betrayal and alienation experienced by incest victims is well borne out by Meiselman (1978) and Reich and Gutierres (1979), both of their studies reporting very high incidences of victims leaving home and running away.

Long-term effects
Research clearly indicates that psychiatric disorder is one of the commonest long-term effects of child sexual abuse. Both Bagley and Ramsay (1987) and Sedney and Brooks (1984) report much higher levels of depression amongst adult women who had been abused in childhood than in the female population as a whole. Briere (1984) reported suicidal tendencies (51 per cent), anxiety attacks (54 per cent), nightmares (72 per cent) and sleeping difficulties (72 per cent). The genesis of fast-developing psychiatric disorder is discernible in Goodwin *et al.*'s (1979) study of hysterical seizures as a sequel to child sexual abuse; and, in Kohan *et al.*'s (1987) disturbing report on sexually abused children who had actually been hospitalized for psychiatric complaints (72 per cent of the children were victims of incest). Herman and Hirschman's (1977) study of psychotherapy patients, sexually molested in childhood, highlights their 'distancing, isolation and negative self images'. James and Meyerding (1977) suggest that prostitution often has its origin in childhood sexual abuse, whilst Benward and Densen-Gerber (1979) claim there is a strong correlation between it and future drug addiction. Numerous other studies have reported serious interpersonal, marital, parenting and socializing difficulties, experienced by adults sexually abused in childhood.

Important variables in researching effects

All these researchers together represent only a fraction of the overall research effort on the effects of child sexual abuse. But very few researchers have, in fact, given due consideration to the multiple variables which have – whether they have been aware of it or not – influenced their findings. Finkelhor (1986) comments on the research into short-term effects: 'At this point, the empirical literature on the initial effects of child sexual abuse would have to be considered sketchy' (p. 152); and, on the long-term effects: 'Findings of long-term impact are especially persuasive' (p. 163). Be that as it may, research into long-term and short-term effects both fail to provide sufficient information about the type of sexual abuse perpetrated against the child, the social and family context in which the abuse took place and, perhaps most important of all, about the ways and means of intervention by agency personnel who became involved. Let's look at this matter more closely, using three contrasting examples of child sexual abuse. One of these will be the case of Sarah and Elizabeth in the first chapter, where we will assume that the father *has* abused the older child as suggested in the medical evidence.

1 Sarah, six-and-a-half years old, has been made to masturbate her father, orally and manually, and has been exposed to pornographic literature. Her father has also 'fingered' her vaginal area. The abuse has occurred regularly and frequently over a six-month period. Sarah has begun to exhibit signs of distress in the classroom. She is becoming more withdrawn and isolated. When the abuse is disclosed, her father denies it. Her mother disbelieves her, condemns and rejects her. Social services complete their intervention by removing Sarah and her sister Elizabeth (see Chapter 1 for precise details of the intervention).
2 Paul, ten years old, has been sexually abused by his mother. He is an only child, and she is a single parent. The abuse consists of mutual mastur-bation, cunnilingus and attempted intercourse. It has taken place over many months. Paul attends special school (non-residential) due to behavioural and educational problems. When the abuse is disclosed, social workers and staff at the school take Paul for a medical examination where the abuse is confirmed. He is immediately made the subject of a place-of-safety order and prevented from having any contact with his mother for two days. She is interviewed by the police after the medical examination, admits to abusing Paul and is arrested and remanded in prison.
3 Mary, five years old, has been sexually abused by a seventeen-year-old child-minder. He has manipulated the child into various sexual activities, fondling, kissing, masturbating and digital penetration. Parents discover the abuse by investigating Mary's discomfort in going to the toilet and her increasing agitation when her parents are about to leave her again with the same child-minder. They are horrified by confirmation of the abuse. They

realize the total innocence of their child, and they accept that they have failed to protect her. They seek professional guidance on this and ensure that it never happens again. They insist that the police do not interview their child about the abuse, and they reject offers of help from social services.

Identity of the perpetrator

It is obvious in these three cases that the sexual abuse by adults is probably having adverse effects upon the emotional, social and psychological lives of the children. But are there not crucial factors in each case which can determine the extent of those adverse effects? For example, the relationships between abusers and children are very different; does that have any bearing on the seriousness of effect? Writers unanimously suggest that sexual abuse by a close relative is far more traumatic in the short term and damaging in the long term than abuse by adults who have had very little contact with the child (Chandler 1982; Groth 1978; Steele and Alexander 1981).

Violence in abuse

In the case of Mary, the perpetrator is not a family member, so might we believe that her abuse is less complicated and serious than the other two? What if the non-family perpetrator engages in a far more serious kind of abuse, e.g. a violent sexual assault or rape (such as the one I've just read about in my local paper, a thirteen-year-old girl dragged into a cemetery by a stranger and raped amongst tombstones); might that not be as serious or more so in its effects than mutual masturbation between child and parent? Finkelhor (1979) seems to say yes. In his development of a measuring scale seeking to establish the degree of trauma endured by victims, he concluded that the use of or lack of 'physical force' was the most crucial single variable. The reality is, of course, that reputable research supporting either of these stances has not yet been carried out, and that researchers have barely begun the task of establishing precisely how single or multiple variables can influence the nature and extent of effect.

Reaction of non-abusing parent

Reactions by abusers, spouses and parent(s) are also very different in the above cases; should that have any bearing on observable effects? The first and third reactions could not be more dissimilar. Sarah's experience of rejection and condemnation by her mother must alarm professionals as much as the abuse itself. Mary's experience, of parents who hold themselves entirely responsible, and who protect their child from any possible trauma caused by an investigation, can only minimize the concern of professionals. The problem for researchers looking into the effects of abuse is not simply the fact that they may not take account of the impact of family context and parental reactions but, even more simply, the matter of who is going to be able to inform them of such contexts. It is highly unlikely that the child herself would be able to convey the major impact of family context or parental reaction, either immediately after disclosure, or twenty years later, from a psychiatric bed. Unless researchers can place themselves at the heart of child sexual-abuse experiences – the heart meaning the family and family members' reactions – as soon as possible after disclosure, the less they will be able to take into account the often overwhelming influence that these factors can have on the effects of the abuse.

The impact of intervention

Finally, the impact of intervention by relevant agencies has got to be considered as an important variable. But who is going to enlighten the researchers? Hardly those professionals who have contemplated the matter and realized the awful possibility that their intervention has actually exacerbated the child's problem. In the case of Sarah and Paul, it is obvious that the professionals have exacerbated their problem. The experiences of Sarah in particular make up a catalogue of disastrous moves, each one of them compounding the damage inflicted by the preceding one, and culminating in the unwitting cruelty of separation and ill-prepared placement in a foster home. Indeed, it may well be argued that the most traumatic experience the child endured, namely, rejection by her mother, was provoked by the actions of the professionals trying to protect her. What then is Sarah likely to be telling the psychiatrist and the researcher in two months' or in twenty years' time? Is there the slightest hope that either could learn of the enormity of the damage inflicted by professionals and their agencies, and of the relationship between that and the symptomology which has brought the child to their attention? Similarly with the case of Paul, whatever trauma was being caused by the sexual abuse perpetrated by his mother, her sudden exposure, disappearance and imprisonment could well have caused even greater trauma. More seriously, the experiences could have rendered his mother incapable of ever caring for him again. Perfectly right too, one might say, but what would Paul say? what would he feel? how would he cope with the devastation inflicted within a matter of hours? the loss of his home and his mother, then his placement in a strange foster or residential home? Might he gradually acquire a debilitating guilt leading to all kinds of symptoms and psychiatric disorder? And would that be made into another statistic supporting the claim about the effects of child sexual abuse?

Research and reality

It would be inaccurate to say that writers and researchers have totally ignored all these often crucial variables which can have a major influence on the effects of child sexual abuse. Indeed, some are actually attempting to classify and prioritize them. For example, Groth (1978) suggests that the greater trauma is likely when the abuse occurs over a long period of time; the perpetrator is a close relative; the abuse involves penetration; it is accompanied by aggression, MacFarlane (1978) adds three more variables: the child participates to some degree; the parents have an unsupportive reaction to disclosure; the child is old enough to be cognizant of the cultural taboos which are being violated. Mrazek and Mrazek (1981) have included all of these except 'the child's participation' in their list of six variables (compiled for the purpose of definition of child sexual abuse). Nevertheless two critical observations may be made: first, reference to effects and the variables which might influence them has the distinct stamp of research writing, i.e. it is cold, methodical and factual, based upon enquiry and observation light years away from the suffering sexually abused children may endure. For example, it is unlikely that researchers could have been made aware of the devastating impact of the anger and coldness in Mrs Williams's face when she first laid eyes on her daughter Sarah, after the disclosure. That kind of pain and its effects are lost in the researcher's terminology: 'the parents have an unsupportive attitude to disclosure'. Second, Chandler's comment that there is no research evidence of the harm done by intervention is probably correct. But do the relevant agencies really need the tragedy of Cleveland to think otherwise? Welfare agencies and their professional staff have enormous difficulties in self-examination, particularly when it is becoming obvious that they may be doing precisely the opposite to what their agency stands for, and the ethics their profession espouses. That is, to help, support and protect; to enhance in some small measure the quality of life of their less fortunate clientele. Researchers too, however, many of them originating from those very same agencies, and/or still heavily related to them, have never shown any inclination to research the unthinkable: that the helpers, the protectors, the supporters, may actually be inflicting more suffering and damage than the abusers. Cleveland has concentrated the mind wonderfully.

The future task for research

The agenda for research into the effects of child sexual abuse is now a little clearer. The quality and method of agency intervention are established as highly influential variables. The purpose of researching this is not to expose professional incompetence or helplessness; on the contrary, one cannot but share a faith that the majority of interventions not only protect victims but alleviate much of the initial trauma of abuse, and that subsequent care and treatment prevent many of the long-term effects this chapter has been exploring. But that is precisely the other side of the coin: researchers have on occasions been misled into concluding that a particular form of abuse, perpetrated against a particular child, has not been as serious in its effects as perhaps previous research would have led them to expect, when the reason for that is that the intervention by protective and judicial agencies was highly sensitive and wholly professional. The aim of researching the variables, therefore, is to establish precisely those attitudes, approaches, skills and techniques most effective in the intervention as a whole.

Research should be more practice and action oriented. That is to say that child sexual abuse should not be treated as if it were merely a newly discovered phenomenon, fascinating to researcher and public alike, offering endless research possibilities, eager publishers, promotion prospects and status. Researchers must ask themselves whether their efforts are to be merely academic, the riskless pursuit of knowledge and understanding, or do they really want to contribute to the efforts of those engaged in the high-risk task of responding to and combating child sexual abuse. If the latter, then they should familiarize themselves with professionals' front-line responsibilities, particularly with initial intervention. They must learn of the various phases of the work and identify where (and why) the greatest difficulties lie. Then they will be able to determine research goals that will be most relevant and useful to the practitioners involved. Many researchers can take credit for their contribution to the exposure of child sexual abuse. It is now imperative that they 'get in on the action' that their findings have generated and widen the focus of their research to include family, environment and the impact of intervening personnel.

Summary and conclusions

Research into child sexual abuse has concentrated upon the prevalence, nature and effect of the abuse. The prevalence statistics are highly unreliable. Differing definitions, population groups and methodologies have been used. These do not necessarily undermine the consistently high prevalence rate which emerges, but they should caution one in interpreting them as indicative of some terrible calamity that has befallen us, with the belief that 50 to 60 per cent of the adult population has been sexually abused in childhood and have suffered long-term emotional and psychological damage as a result. Research studies on prevalence have assumed an authority and status totally incompatible with their real worth. There is no indication that such studies have contributed anything towards enabling social workers and other professionals to respond more effectively to child sexual abuse. The major contribution of prevalence figures has, regrettably, been political; intensifying the public's abhorrence of child sexual abuse, thereby making it more difficult for the public to accept the need for developing alternative, non-punitive strategies for coping with it.

There has been much research effort made to identify those children who are in greatest risk of being sexually abused. The research has been invariably retrospective in nature, i.e. it has relied upon adults remembering the details and circumstances of being sexually abused in childhood. This research is predominantly American in origin, the victims mostly women, and the type of abuse mostly incest. The conclusions, therefore, may not be applicable to child populations as a whole in America itself and may be even less so in Britain. The research has consistently identified the ten-to-twelve-year-old child, whose parent(s) are absent or in conflict, as most at risk, but the population groups which have been researched, and the retrospective methodology, have allowed researchers to ignore particular groups of children who may be in much greater risk, i.e. children with special needs and mentally handicapped children.

The research into the effects of child sexual abuse is heavily flawed. Some researchers have demonstrated an awareness of numerous and important variables, but no great effort has been made to establish the precise influence of these variables. One variable which has never been considered in any research may be the most significant one of all, namely, how agencies like social services, police and the judiciary respond to the abuse. There is ample evidence available for researchers now to demonstrate how influential this variable is. Apart from the intrinsic merit of researching it, the research would be most welcome and useful to individual professionals, and to training establishments. The training and the practice of professionals who intervene in child sexual abuse are far more in their infancy than is the research that has exposed it. Research that explores practice and training implications therefore can make a vital contribution to the development of new, and much needed, alternative intervention strategies.

6
Towards a social-work categorization of child sexual abuse

Introduction

Social work has an unenviable compulsion to immerse itself in all forms of human misery, to relieve the victims of any suffering they may endure and to seek as much knowledge and expertise to enable it to enlighten and inform – even educate and train – its many members and related professionals. This is a wholly edifying tendency, though highly impractical. The most obvious consequence is that most social workers learn very little about anything and often feel that the level of expertise they gain equips them for nothing. No doubt, if some terrifying new disease or disaster were to be inflicted upon the general population in the forthcoming months, the profession's leaders and managers would find an important role for social workers. Social workers themselves would feel obliged not only to gain expertise about that particular problem, but also to respond to every single referral involving it, irrespective of the severity of suffering endured by the victims. It is important to remember this chronic disposition of the profession in the current debates following Cleveland. Before that tragedy, individual social workers were repeatedly exposed as untrained, inexperienced and incompetent, in their long-established, most important statutory duty of the protection of abused children (DHSS 1982). Then came the phenomenal increase in child sexual-abuse cases and the startling research claims that as many as one in five children in the general population may be being sexually abused. One would think that previous condemnations of the social-work response to child abuse generally would have cautioned leaders and managers into declaring that social services and other agencies might have some difficulty in taking on this additional role of rescuing upwards of three million children! But it didn't. Instead, leaders and managers, educators and

trainers, conveyed the reassuring message to the public at large that social
workers knew all about child sexual abuse, that they had a paramount duty
to protect children from it and that they would respond effectively to every
single case brought to their attention. Pervasive throughout this utterly
laughable reassurance was a regrettable lack of discrimination in thinking
and proposed actions. The single most influential factor in the tragedy of
Cleveland and in similar tragedies elsewhere is the total lack of a meaningful
social-work categorization of child sexual abuse. The social-work profession
is reluctant to categorize anything. To categorize means to prioritize. In
child sexual abuse, that means to recognize that there are many different
types of abuse perpetrated against many different ages and types of children,
and that some of these abuses are far more serious than others, more serious
in their damaging long-term effects, and in the challenges they pose to the
social workers who have statutory obligations towards the victims. This
chapter will identify and explore the essential components of a social-work
categorization of child sexual abuse. These are protection, the family and
social context and resources.

In exploring each of these applied to individual cases, we will quickly
realize that social workers cannot and must not attempt to respond to every
single child sexual-abuse referral that comes their way; that social workers
have a clear statutory obligation to intervene in certain cases but, equally
clearly, have an obligation *not* to intervene in other cases; that categorizing
and prioritizing child sexual abuse demand as much scrutiny of ourselves and
of our agencies' resources as they do of the nature and extent of the abuse
the child has endured.

The necessity, value and implication of a social-work categorization

In the light of Cleveland's condemnation of the lack of multi-disciplinary
co-operation, readers may ponder the 'necessity' of categorizing child sexual
abuse from a purely social-work perspective. There are, however, convincing reasons for doing so. First, the Cleveland report (Butler-Sloss 1988), as
have many other preceding reports, has once again exposed the myth about
multi-disciplinary co-operation which has taken root since the Maria
Colwell report of 1974, i.e. that multi-disciplinary co-operation is a natural,
mutually desirable process, and thereby easy to attain. Yet, far from
observing professionals from the different agencies sitting together and
reaching consensus in understanding, approach and strategy, the public has
annually witnessed the most undignified battles, not just between different
professional groups, but, more ominously, between the same professionals
within the same agencies. (For example, who would have believed the level
of mutual contempt and animosity exhibited between medical personnel
before, during and after the publication of Cleveland?) The Cleveland
report however, identifies the single most important cause of this sorry state

of affairs: 'Each agency needs to have formulated the basic principles and frameworks of its own practice . . .' (p. 54). This means that each agency (and the profession associated with it) would be well advised to clarify its own perspective on child sexual abuse, its underlying philosophical and professional conviction about differing aspects of such abuse, and on how their perspective determines what are the most difficult cases, and where the greatest challenges lie with those cases; in short, to clarify its own thinking and reasoning on how it would categorize and prioritize the child sexual-abuse cases it encounters. Apart from the multi-disciplinary advantages, Moore (1985; 17) reminds us of the more important beneficiary:

> Abusing families would get a better service if each discipline were much clearer about its role in abusive situations, and more sure of what was its own specialist contribution.

The second reason for categorizing from a social-work perspective is the major contribution it makes to the overall multi-disciplinary effort. Social workers work mainly in the homes and in the communities of the sexually abused child. They are heavily involved at the outset in the referral, investigative and intervention phases, all of which are likely to include family and community. They are primarily responsible for providing alternative accommodation for the child, and for maintaining the child's links with its family and community. Their training and professional code emphasize the importance of their engaging whole families. Their statutory obligations are actually aimed towards whole families. They therefore have opportunities to observe aspects of the community and family contexts of the abuse which other professionals probably do not have. A social-worker categorization must not therefore be interpreted as anti-multidisciplinary. It should be recognized for what it is, an exercise that enables social workers to share with their colleagues of other disciplines their wide-ranging perceptions of the nature and context of the abuse, and of the challenges and resources needed to effectively combat it. This can only be a major contribution towards understanding, and towards the necessary intervention (preferably) carried out in collaboration with those colleagues.

The implication of any categorization is, of course, that some forms of sexual abuse will be perceived to be less serious or demanding than others, and that certain professional groups, including social workers, have no statutory role to play in the prevention of and in dealing with the effects of particular forms of abuse. That is a reality that social services in particular has failed to grasp in the past few years, causing immense frustration amongst staff, and, doing no good at all to sexually abused children and families alike.

The principal function of categorization

In all previous child sexual-abuse literature and training, categorization initially meant nothing more than a listing and naming of particular child sexual-abuse acts, e.g. inappropriate touching, petting, kissing, sexual embracing, exposing, masturbation, cunnilingus, fellatio, intercourse, buggery, etc. More sophisticated categorizations followed, with the identification of important variables determining the seriousness and the effects of the abuse (CIBA 1984; Finkelhor 1984, 1986; Mrazek and Mrazek 1981). A social-work categorization, however, goes far beyond the mere identification of child sexual-abuse acts, and of the variables which determine its effects. It is primarily concerned with the nature of the challenge which particular aspects and components of the whole child-abusing situation poses for the worker. It also addresses the hitherto ignored question of resources needed to combat the abuse without inflicting further damage upon the child.

But what precisely is the function of categorization? It is, to put it bluntly, to professionalize thinking and responses to that most misused term, 'child sexual abuse'. Professionals, writers, trainers and commentators have all indulged in the widespread and repetitive, and wholly inappropriate, use of the term. It has been misused primarily through the aim of evoking feeling rather than provoking discriminating thought. It seems to have had the inevitable function of justifying any preceding argument about any particular type of abuse, and any drastic action proposed in conclusion: 'child sexual abuse' – horror of horrors, do what they must! The principal function of categorization, therefore, is to provoke an instant, detailed, and comprehensive conceptual framework in response to the term 'child sexual abuse' to facilitate the necessary differentiation amongst its many types and component parts. The consequence of that can only be the soundest basis for action, the realization of the precise kind of action or inaction that is required and, most important of all, whether or not the protective agencies have the resources to ensure that any action will be effective. We can best begin the task by highlighting the extent of differences in some actual cases.

1   Joan is fourteen years old. She is accosted by a middle-aged male streaker, as she returns home from a friend. She is very disturbed by this experience. The perpetrator is unknown and is not apprehended. A few weeks later, the same thing happens again. Joan is terrified. Her parents are angry and distraught and thereafter ensure that she does not return home alone again.

2   Jane is four years old, and her sister, Marie, is two. They have been sexually abused by a sixteen-year-old male baby-sitter. This has happened frequently, each Saturday evening. They have been manipulated into indulging in manual and oral masturbation and have been subjected to digital penetration. The disclosure is made at Jane's nursery, through her drawings and conversations with nursery staff. Social services are informed. The police become involved. The parents are horrified when they learn about the abuse. They threaten to 'kill' the perpetrator and vow that they will never leave their children in the care of baby-sitters again.

3   Joanne is twelve years old. She has a sister aged fourteen and two

stepbrothers, Paul, aged eight, and Simon, aged five. Joanne discloses that on one occasion, six months previously, she was sexually abused by her stepfather. He attempted intercourse with her, compelled her to masturbate him orally and manually and paid her to keep quiet. Joanne's stepfather has a well-paid secure job. The family have a reasonable standard of living. All the children function well, socially and education-ally. Their physical health is excellent. They are often in contact with extended family members. Joanne tells her mother about the abuse. Her mother immediately takes her child to the GP. He explains that he has to inform social services. She begs him not to, but he insists, trying to convince her that it is the right thing to do.

4 Martin is fifteen years old. He has been sexually abused by his mother for the past four years. Their relationship is totally symbiotic and incestuous. Martin's stepfather has gradually learnt about the abuse since marrying Martin's mother, two years previously. It seems that he has not disclosed primarily because of his own weakness, and his fear of the consequential shame, stigma and possible charge for being an accomplice. Martin's emotional, psychological, social and educational life have been seriously impaired by the sexual abuse, and he has been assessed for special education. The abuse first came to light when Martin was being questioned by police about numerous petty thefts he'd been indulging in. He is medically examined. His mother is interviewed. He is removed to a children's home through a place-of-safety order. He soon yearns to return to his mother. He is deeply depressed in the centre, unable to mix with other residents, frequently bullied, and displaying suicidal tendencies. His mother visits him every day and begs staff to let him return. She denies that she has ever abused him in any way, yet she discloses that she was sexually and physically abused often in her own childhood. Her GP reports that she has become something of a physical and mental wreck since the disclosure was first made. Martin later clams up when again approached by staff about his mother's abuse of him. Her husband denies that he knew Martin was being sexually abused, yet he acknowledges the possibility that it might have been happening without his knowing.

The uniqueness of child sexual-abuse experiences

There are many questions that one might want to ask about each of these cases, but for the moment let's assume that the information provided is fact. What is also fact is the uniqueness of each case, the victims, the perpetrators, the family context and, probably, the effects of each abuse. The problem for practitioners and those who purport to train them is that if they do acknowledge the uniqueness of all aspects of each of these abuses, then it is also an acknowledgement that each of them may require entirely different approaches, attitudes and strategies. But the reality is, for example, that no one has a clue about the 'right' approach, attitude and strategy for dealing with fourteen-year-old girls repeatedly accosted by streakers. No doubt, her GP, psychiatrist, social worker and teachers would have much sympathy for her and would offer endless comfort and support. But would anyone of them be applying an established, tested and effective strategy that would guarantee Joan's rapid recovery? Such a strategy doesn't exist, for the simple reason that the categorization in which all aspects of Joan's unique experiences could be identified, and their effects anticipated, doesn't exist either.

Assessing whether or not to intervene

In Joan's case, however, there really isn't a need for any strategy. It's the least problematic of the cases. Her parents are capable of protecting her far more effectively than any agency. As for social services and statutory responsibility, there isn't the slightest need for social workers' intervention. Unless they or any other professionals have nothing else to do, the case should be ignored, and attention given to far more numerous and deserving cases. Thus we have taken a tiny but nonetheless significant step forward, not just in social-work categorization, but also in social-work definition. Yes, child sexual abuse can include the traumatic experiences endured by children confronted by male adult streakers, but, comparatively speaking, these traumas and their effects are infinitely less serious and challenging than many other categories which social workers are more likely to be encountering.

In the case of Jane and Marie, initial revulsion at the thought of two infants' being repeatedly sexually abused by their teenage carer should give way to a more optimistic awareness that, *comparatively speaking*, their situation too is much less serious than that of the vast majority of sexually abused children with whom social workers become statutorily involved. There are numerous observations which would support this view. First, whatever the physical, psychological and emotional experiences the children had whilst being abused, it was not having any visible adverse effect upon their physical, psychological and emotional development. No doubt, had the abuse continued, it would have degenerated into worse, more damaging forms of abuse, and the children's development would have become seriously and very obviously impaired. But the fact that the disclosure emerged through the curiosity of the teacher, rather than through any physical or psychological discomfort of the child, indicates that investigation and apprehension of the offender took place long before that. Second, there is no more reassuring sound to a social worker's ear than the genuine anguish and anger of parents who discover that their children have been sexually abused. Part of their disgust and anger, of course, stems from the realization of their own lack of caution in the choice of a child-minder. But it is precisely this realization that is likely to provide a far greater safeguard to the children than anything that social services has to offer. As for prosecution of the offender, parental opposition to any attempt to interview these children should be respected. Not just for the sound ethical reason of respect for parents, but because, more pragmatically, both parents and children will need a great deal of time and a very relaxed atmosphere before they are psychologically capable of providing police with the co-operation required. Social services has no statutory role in this case and, having reassured the parents that sexual abuse of toddlers by teenage child-minders is one of the most common forms of abuse situations, and praised them for their very reasonable, justifiable responses (of wanting to kill the child minder!), social workers should make a hasty exit from the case and return to their far more demanding child sexual-abuse work. They will certainly find that in the next case.

Abuse by a parent or carer

The case of Joanne lies within a category infinitely more complex and demanding than the previous two. Social services have a very clear obligation to intervene. Joanne has been sexually assaulted, bribed to keep it a secret and is still partially under the care of that same perpetrator. Joanne needs to be protected from the possibility of any form of abuse occurring again, and from the consequences of her disclosure. Pre-Cleveland, there would have been nothing unusual about the compulsory removal of Joanne, achieving the objectives of protecting her from possible revenge consequences of her disclosure of the first abuse, and ensuring that she is not subjected to any further abuse (also, of course, wholly justifying mother's reluctance for anyone to know!). Now, however, professionals must contemplate the seemingly more sensible alternative of getting the perpetrator removed. Surely that must be a more preferable way of achieving those objectives.

This much heralded new strategy, the removal of the perpetrator, is as unspecified and uncategorized, as the term 'child sexual abuse' itself. Does it mean an instant police interrogation of the perpetrator? and, if he confesses, his immediate removal, prosecution, conviction and imprisonment? Nothing could be better calculated to inflict massive suffering upon the family, ensuring the most debilitating guilt in the victim, and years of futile counselling and therapy by the professionals. The question of whether it is in *anybody*'s interest for the perpetrator to be removed, with or without his agreement, can only be answered after a rigorous assessment of the family context of the abuse, and in knowing what will be the likely fate of the perpetrator after he is removed. Particular attention has to be given to exploring the nature of, and the contribution that context – including the perpetrator – makes to the social, educational, emotional and psychological development of the victim. And it must also include an honest, realistic assessment of the resources of social services and other welfare agencies for their attempts to support the family during the short- or long-term removal of the perpetrator. Such assessments are at the core of a social-work categorization of child sexual abuse, and we must therefore dwell upon this particular case a little longer.

Investigations upon which a social-work categorization is made

Protection

Protection is the primary concern in any assessment that aims towards a social-work categorization of child sexual abuse. Let us look at the main lines of enquiry which this protective function necessitates:

1 Is Joanne's mother aware of any occasion in the past when she suspected that Joanne or any of her other children were being sexually abused? Can she recall any of her children's behaviour or distress for which there was no explanation? Has she ever noticed any change in the relationship between her children and father/stepfather? (All of these questions are based upon the assumption that isolated incidents of child sexual abuse are rare and, that if one child in the family is being abused, it is likely that others are as well. The more suspicion and disclosure therefore, the more need for 'protection'.)

2 Why was mother, Joanne's primary protector, unable to find out about the abuse until six months after it occurred? Had she ever been sexually abused in childhood? What kind of a relationship does she have with Joanne? Is it an emotionally distant one? Has Joanne unsuccessfully attempted to tell her mother about the abuse on another occasion? What has been the effect of the disclosure upon her present relationship with Joanne? Is there any indication of hostility or jealousy towards the child, as a consequence of her discovery that her husband sought sexual gratification from her own daughter. Have any ambivalent feelings developed towards her husband since the disclosure?

3 What is the history of relationships between husband and wife? How sexually fulfilling has it been for either? Have their hopes and aspirations in marrying a second time been satisfied? What were the main difficulties in reconstituting a new family? Did Joanne or any of the other children rebel? Did Joanne increasingly withdraw from the family? How did they cope with it? Was it ever a source of friction between them? Is there any indication of Joanne being scapegoated?

4 Does the perpetrator have any previous record of offences against children? How does he recall his abuse against Joanne? Does he deny it? Does he attempt to blame her in any way? Has he any remorse about what he has done, or does he display only fear and denial? Does he attempt character assassination of Joanne in his defence? What attitude and feeling is he now displaying towards Joanne in the light of her disclosure and his wife's belief that he has sexually abused her?

Quite clearly, this particular thrust of enquiry on 'protection' revolves around the character, attitude, history and existing relationships of the parents. This will elicit valuable information enabling the social worker to assess the risk of Joanne being abused again and the likely adverse consequences of her having disclosed that she was abused previously. The next major thrust of enquiry concentrates upon influences and contributions of the wider family and social context. It is important primarily because of its value in assessing the likely consequences of a decision to remove the child.

The family and social context

Abuse + what?
Joanne has been abused in this family, but what else is the family doing to her? Is there anything in the family that she herself would think and feel more important than the abuse perpetrated against her? The following lines of enquiry may help to answer that question:

1 What can you observe and learn about Joanne's physical, emotional, social, psychological and educational life? How much normality or progress in any of these spheres derives from the care, love, security, material well-being that is provided by her mother, stepfather, siblings, neighbourhood friends, extended family, and her community?
2 Does Joanne value the presence and care her mother offers her? Why? What is Joanne's perception of the nature, quality and extent of care her mother provides?
3 Does Joanne value anything at all about the perpetrator? Has he contributed anything to her well-being? Was he, before abusing her, a major improvement on the father she lost, or on the fatherless existence before he came along? Was he a genuine substitute father, contributing to her education, her hobbies, interests, sports and social life?
4 Does Joanne value the reconstituted family, the 'whole' family, in preference to a single-parent family? Does she value its stronger economic base and the increased standard of living it has brought?
5 Did Joanne welcome the arrival of two stepchildren? Did she derive any pleasure or status or influence from their arrival? Does she have any close affinity with either of them or with her sister?
6 What effect has the abuse had upon Joanne's physical, emotional, social, psychological and educational development?
7 Finally, if the perpetrator were removed, what does one think the effect would be on Joanne herself? Would she feel relieved and secure? Would she feel sorry or guilty in any way? Would she feel that the unity of the family had been destroyed? Would she dread the consequences within the family itself, the economic and relationship consequences, the social and educational consequences? Would she rapidly acquire a disturbing realization that her mother now has to cope with four children alone, and would she become increasingly guilt ridden and fearful because it is her

disclosure that has caused her two stepbrothers to lose their natural father?

This particular thrust of enquiry does not seek to minimize the abuse suffered by Joanne, but it does aim to expose the precise family and social circumstances in which the abuse took place. The events in Cleveland were partially caused by social-work forgetfulness that such enquiries are merely routine in any abuse investigation. The only explanation can be that social workers allowed themselves to be overwhelmed, to become obsessed merely with establishing the facts about the abuse, and the abuse only. It should be noticed that, though this particular investigation is mainly concerned with the family and social context, it is an investigation carried out solely through the perceptions and feelings (and the observations the social worker makes) of Joanne herself. The question then arises: if one is impressed and reassured about certain aspects of the family and social life as manifest in the appearance, character and attainments of Joanne, is there any justification for weighing this against the very serious sexual abuse perpetrated against her. Or is the abuse so repugnant, so seriously criminal, so damaging that the abused and abuser have to be separated in some way? The answer to these questions brings us to the third and final thrust of enquiry which is to explore agency resources which may facilitate this separation and enable social workers to cope more adequately with the difficulties which it creates.

The resources issue

What have resources to do with a social-work categorization of child sexual abuse? Each case of abuse requires one or more of a number of appropriate responses from professional staff, the responses of thought, attitude, approach, action, joint action with other agencies, the availability and use of numerous facilities and aids, etc. All these are necessary and sought-after resources. The seriousness of each act of abuse can be measured by its effects. In the previous chapter we learnt that the way agencies and their professional staff respond can determine effects. For example, initial perceptions and intervention, the instant removal of the child, hasty attempts at disclosure work, inadequate or non-existing fostering facilities – all these can significantly worsen the effects. Excellent resources, on the other hand, mean high-quality responses which can minimize the effects. Social-work managers should know the quality and training of their staff and the quantity and quality of their additional resources. These factors will be taken into consideration in categorizing cases according to their challenges and their complexities. For example, if social workers (or even a child sexual-abuse team) have no experience or expertise in working with father perpetrators who exercise major influence over families, such a case may pose insurmountable problems. If staff, however, have considerable experience and skills in dealing with three-to-five-year-old sexually abused children and their families and have numerous facilities, i.e. suitable rooms and equipment with which to supplement the work, such a case is not likely to present anything like the same difficulty.

In the case under discussion the removal of the child or the removal of the perpetrator each demands different types of resources. The former demands the provision of adequate, specialized, well-equipped and well-staffed residential facilities or the availability of a placement with foster parents experienced in fostering sexually abused children. The use of either of these alternative accommodations require careful planning, initial contacts and introductions, and the guarantee of frequent contact with the non-abusing parent and, if the child and mother so request, supervised access with the abusing parent. The removal of the perpetrator, on the other hand, will necessitate intensive exploration with mother of the marital, social and economic consequences, and of the care and support of the remaining children. This will be a time of major crisis for all family members, a crisis that will intensify in the weeks ahead. The social worker therefore, having been instrumental in the investigation which has led to the crisis, has the obligation to commit him or herself totally to the family during this period, to give whatever counselling or practical help is necessary. (All these provisions highlight the ethical aspects of the resources issue, as discussed in Chapter 4.)

These three major thrusts of enquiry, revolving around the issues of protection, family and social context, and resources, should enable us to categorize and prioritize cases with precision. They also lay the foundations of strategy for dealing with cases. We will now move on to our final case, that of Martin. There is an additional thrust of enquiry to be made in this case. It is not merely a case of formidable challenges and complexity, but one of very real dangers as well. These dangers have got to be explored and assessed.

Incest: a category of danger

Protection

It is somewhat ironic in this case that, when the abused child is removed from the perpetrator and the quite devastating abuse which she has inflicted upon him, the challenges confronting those entrusted with Martin's care increase significantly. Here the question of how to protect Martin from further abuse, and from the consequences of the initial disclosure, would appear to have been unintentionally answered for us. His mother cannot abuse him as long as he remains in residential care, nor can she wreak some kind of revenge in response to his disclosure. There is little need here to pursue the protection issue as rigorously as we have done in the case of Joanne, because it is abundantly clear that Martin would probably endure further abuse and revenge if he were returned. Such protection as is being provided, however, can reassure no one.

The family and social context

Abuse + what?

The assessment and school reports have stated that Martin's emotional, psychological and social life have been seriously impaired. There can be little doubt that this is partially, if not wholly, due to the sexual abuse. But it is also clear that other aspects of the home and family context compound the abuse. This is a depressing and challenging case for many reasons; the main reason is that there is so little of GOOD in the family as it presently exists and functions. This family is immersed in pathology, cruelty, fear and massive self-deceptions. In its present form it has nothing to offer Martin except food, shelter and sustained damaging abuse that will eventually place him in a psychiatric ward. Yet he desperately wants to return, and his mother is reported to be rapidly disintegrating because there is little prospect of his return. How can that be, and how is it interpreted in an assessment of the home and family context?

Incest cases like these are uniquely challenging, because the abuse has usually been occurring over a long time, increasing in frequency and in severity, and becoming ingrained in the family pattern of relationships, and so pathologically functional for all family members. The frequency, duration and function of the abuse is fundamental in any appreciation of the consequences of removing the victim. The present-day abuse which has come to light is only the end product of numerous and complex marital, psychological and sexual processes. The origins of these lie in the family's history. These processes have been strengthening and intensifying every hour of every day over many weeks and months. Suddenly, without warning, they are invaded by hostile external forces, i.e. police and social services. The pivot around which these processes revolve and upon which they are totally dependent (namely Martin) is removed. Why then the danger?

Abuse + danger

Imagine yourself as an incestuous abuser of your fifteen-year-old son or daughter. The abuse has been occurring over a long period of time. You have become more and more dependent upon it. The increasing pleasure and dependency is marred only by the thought of being caught out, and the ghastly consequences: you imagine the expressions on your friends' and colleagues' faces, the local newspaper headlines, the loss of job, imprisonment, the permanent shame, stigma and penury. Imagine also that you reach the point of believing that you cannot live without this incestuous relationship, and that your victim, in allowing you to abuse him or her repeatedly, seems to be saying exactly the same thing. How then do you think you might react to your own exposure?

Within a twenty-mile radius of Leeds, between the years 1982 and 1986, no less than seven deaths (three suicides and four murders) occurred in incestuous families, after disclosure and the involvement of relevant agencies. In Cleveland, in the first six months of 1987, there were two suicides by men accused of sexually abusing their related children. Given the above imaginary scenario, it isn't difficult to see why. The uncomfortable fact is that many incestuous abusers are convinced that life isn't worth living when they've been exposed. Sad as that may be, it is not the primary concern of social workers. Of far greater concern are those abusers who are also convinced that *the victims' lives are not worth living after they (the abusers) have been exposed.* (In Leeds, one of the murders was that of a fourteen-year-old girl, the victim of sexual abuse, by her stepfather, the alleged perpetrator. He then killed himself and his wife. In another case just outside Leeds, the alleged perpetrator repeatedly stabbed his wife, then hung himself.) Here then is the grimmest, most dangerous assessment arena of all, and social workers must know that it is precisely their legitimate action of removal which has increased the risks of suicide and murder considerably.

Trying to assess these risks is not a job for the faint hearted, nor for the inexperienced; even less so is it a job for a single worker. But social workers have a major contribution to make nonetheless, because they are conveniently placed, involved with and mobile between residential home, foster home and family home. They are therefore in an ideal position to recognize risks, and to recommend action that will minimize them. Martin's increasing alienation in the residential home is clearly a high-risk sign. The inability of staff to reach out to him and his increasing clamour to get home are others. The most worrying development, however, is the mental state of his mother. The relationship between mother and son does seem to be a purely symbiotic one, one of total mutual dependence. If further assessment proves this to be the case, then there is little possibility of halting, even slowing, their deteriorating conditions – at least not while they are separated. No doubt, both mother and son will rapidly reach the point of believing that life just isn't worth living. In this case of a symbiotic tie, however, there is no great reassurance in knowing that we can at least prevent Martin from killing himself; his mother's suicide, for which he will inevitably hold himself responsible, will probably have the effect of rendering him a living corpse. The principal consequence of this kind of intervention, therefore, would be to place Martin in a psychiatric ward more quickly than his mother's abuse would have done.

This assessment casts serious doubts on the wisdom of removing Martin in the first instance. The removal protects him from further sexual abuse, but it unleashes physiological and psychological forces over which no one is likely to have any control. Martin has been grossly abused over a very long period of time. He has been seriously damaged in the process. It is highly unlikely that he will be any more seriously damaged if he is left within the home until such time as professionals can assess and formulate an effective strategy for rescuing him without provoking suicidal or murderous deeds that threaten to destroy the whole family. Even without the threat of death and murder, however, the removal of Martin still seems to be folly. This is partially to do with the fact that he cannot mentally or physically cope with an immediate unplanned move to an alien and threatening environment. But it is also to do with the wider issue of social-service resources which might be mobilized in the attempt to enable him to cope.

The resources issue

This case necessitates a highly intelligent, sensitive and flexible management, sophisticated multi-disciplinary co-operation, particularly between police and social services, specially qualified child sexual-abuse social workers with a particular interest and experience in working with teenage male incest victims, their abusing mothers and their families, and special residential and fostering resources. Most social workers reading this may now have to be picked off the floor where they've lain in convulsive fits of laughter, their own experiences convincing them that the mere suggestion of such luxurious resources is one big bad joke. The problem with that attitude, however, is that it discourages one from seriously contemplating the different type of resources that different categories of sexually abused children need, both from the agency, and from the individual professional(s) assigned to the case. The resources may not indeed be available and probably are not in most social-services offices, but social workers should nevertheless know precisely what they mean by 'necessary resources' for individual cases and be able to enlighten their management about the consequences of such resources not being available. In Martin's case the following queries on the resources are necessary:

1 How much collective experience do your and other agencies in the area have of this particular type of abuse?
2 Do you, your supervisor, team, management, accept that this is a particularly dangerous type of case? Is there a carefully worked-out strategy, either within your department or your and other agencies, for coping with this kind of dangerousness, from the time of initial referral, through investigation, intervention and case-conference phase?
3 Do you have any ideological or philosophical reluctance to work with a mother–son incest case?
4 Can you accept that Martin may be safer if left temporarily in the abusing situation? Can you cope with the thought that he is almost certainly being sexually abused again in that situation?
5 If, when Martin was removed, you sensed the high risk which has been discussed above, are you more likely to involve yourself in the family dynamics which generate such risks, exploring ways in which they can be minimized or are you more likely to withdraw from family members, seeking the security of your statutory action of removal, and the certainty that he will at least not be abused by his mother again?
6 Do you have the experience, skills and knowledge to engage this family meaningfully, to engage mother and son in particular?
7 What is the nature and quality of relationships between your own agency

and the police? Is there an effective, joint working relationship? Do both agencies and their senior personnel share an understanding about the origins and causes of child sexual abuse? Is it possible or likely that they would perceive and respond to Martin's case similarly? Would the police accept that there is the very real risk of catastrophe, if they adopt a merely prosecurity and punitive response?

Prioritizing and ignoring: the really difficult task

Sufficient attention has been given to each of these cases to enable us to prioritize them in respect of the challenges and demands they make of social workers. A reminder of the cases:

1 Martin: mother–son incest.
2 Joanne: attempted intercourse by stepfather.
3 Jane and Marie: oral masturbation by teenage male child-minder.
4 Joan: twice exposed to flasher.

The suggestion has been made that, as far as social workers and social services are concerned, the third and fourth cases can be ignored. Social services have no statutory responsibility to become involved and, unless the parents are seeking social-work help, any involvement by social workers would be an infringement of parental rights.

Irrespective of any ethical justification for not becoming involved, however, there is the very pragmatic consideration that social workers simply do not have the time to spare for usurping the rights and duties of parents well capable and willing to carry out those duties themselves. During the panic stricken years of 1985–7, social-services departments were inundated with quite ludicrous child sexual-abuse referrals, causing front-line staff to waste countless hours, energy and expense in investigation, when their professional instinct told them that they should not have been investigating. Of course, some of these referrals might have been concealing the most horrendous kind of abuse; but so too might every household in the land! The great advantage of systematic professional categorizing is the authority and confidence it gives one for the necessary task of discriminating, and occasionally ignoring.

Categorization

A diagrammatic framework for assessing protection

Having examined and emphasized the differences in child sexual-abuse cases and looked at the numerous challenges they pose to social services and individual social workers, we are now in a position to construct some simple reference grids which will enable one to categorize and to prioritize more

Table 6.1   Protection: parents, their role, attitudes and reactions

Type of abuse	Did either parent or carer participate in the abuse?	Did either facilitate or contribute in any way?	Did either approve?
Soliciting			
Pornography			
Exhibitionism (Case of Joan)	NO	NO	NO
Inappropriate touching			
Kissing			
Sexually embracing or fondling			
Masturbation			
Cunnilingus			
Fellatio (case of Jane and Marie)	NO	NO	NO
Attempted intercourse (case of Joanne)	YES	YES	YES
Intercourse			
Buggery			
Father–daughter incest			
Father–son buggery			
Mother–son incest (case of Martin)	YES	YES	YES
Maternal Neonatal incest			

Did either criticize or condemn the child?	Did either or both take immediate steps to protect the child?	Did either or both alert the police, NSPCC, social services or other agencies?	Did either both condemn the abuse and abuser unequivocally?
NO	YES	YES (both)	YES (both)
NO	YES (both)	YES (both)	YES (both)
NO	YES (mother)	YES (mother)	YES (mother)
NO	NO	NO	NO

systematically than previously. Categorization is constructed around crucially significant contexts, the nature and quality of which determine the effects and outcome of the abuse, and the role and responsibilities (if any) of the social worker. The first and most important context is *the protection of the child*. The reliability of that context as a categorizing tool depends almost wholly upon the quality of the parental/carer foundations, i.e. the precise relationship between the parents/'carers and the sexual abuse inflicted upon their child. Social work must test out these foundations as comprehensively as possible. The grid reference in table 6.1 may help; it includes the four cases we've already discussed.

These categories of abuse have been arranged in a way which one may accept as moving from the least serious, i.e. soliciting and pornography, neither of which involves any physical contact, to the most serious, i.e. maternal neonatal incest, a particularly horrific and very damaging kind of abuse perpetrated by young mothers on their new-born male sons (Chasnoff *et al*. 1986). However, the answers to the questions asked in the remaining seven columns could easily upset this particular prioritizing. With the exception of the last four categories, which have to remain extremely serious in any categorization, the effects of the remaining twelve abuses, and the challenges which they do or do not pose, will be determined largely by the answers given. This means, for example, that the least damaging (to the client) and the least challenging (for the social worker) are not necessarily those at the top of the list, but rather those that answer 'Yes' in the first four columns (i.e. the parent(s) participated in the abuse, facilitated it, approved of it and condemned the victim), and, 'No' in the last three columns (i.e. the parent(s) did not protect, did not inform agencies, did not condemn the perpetrator). Joan's encounter with an exhibitionist, therefore, would have been an entirely different (more serious) type of case, if her father had been the exhibitionist, and her mother had facilitated it in some way, and if neither of them disproved of it, and if both of them condemned Joan for making such a fuss about it. Alternatively, even the usually very serious and challenging father–daughter incest may not be so serious and will be a lot less challenging, if mother immediately reported on finding out, offered love and comfort to her daughter, took steps to ensure her protection and condemned the abuse and abuser unequivocably.

The fact that nearly all these answers in the columns above are unknown when social workers and police officers receive a child sexual-abuse referral should not deter the former, in particular, from seeking out the answers. They are as important as getting a disclosure from the child that abuse actually did take place and worthy of the same effort and patience. Nor is it enough merely to get yes/no answers; the reasons behind those answers must be sought, and their implications for the general welfare of the child. This brings us to the next crucial task in the categorization of child sexual abuse, assessing the family and social context of the abuse, through direct observations of the child's physical, emotional, psychological, social and educational life.

A diagrammatic framework for assessing the family and social context

One of the most galling features in the media response to Cleveland was the constant lecturing of social workers about the need to look 'at the whole child . . . its family and social life etc. : . . .' Unfortunately the incidence of allegedly sexually abused children who were not looked at in this respect reached frightening proportions. Cleveland demonstrated that this basic social-work principle and practice can be very easily discarded, despite the painful and periodic reminders from dozens of child-abuse inquiry reports of the disastrous consequences which can ensue. In the case of Beckford and similar tragedies social workers deluded themselves about the nature and extent of the suffering those children were enduring, because they relied only on passing observation of the child's appearance. In Cleveland, however, it seems as though no significance at all was given by paediatricians or social workers to observations of any kind, other than those made of the anal and genital areas. The inevitable counter-argument has since been made, that the family and social context is secondary to *the protection of the child*, and that spending time exploring the former is merely a search for some good in the family, to counterbalance and to minimize its sexual-abusing evil; that is to say, that, although the child has been abused in the family, there are many strengths and values in that family which are vitally important to the child. That may well be the case, and social workers should thoroughly explore such a possibility. But it is not the main reason for assessing the family and social context. In fact, it is almost the opposite to the main reason which is to observe and assess whether or not there is valuable evidence to substantiate the allegation of sexual abuse, and to explore the possibility of the child also being subjected to numerous other types of abuse, very much related to, or stemming from, the sexual abuse itself. It is for this reason that assessment of the family context of sexual abuse is *not* carried out primarily through interviewing and engaging the family, but rather, through numerous professionals' observations of the allegedly sexually abused child. In observing the child's physical, emotional, psychological, social and educational life, one can learn a great deal more about the effects of the sexual abuse she may be enduring, and about the family and social context in which that abuse is or is not occurring.

Here are two very contrasting cases. We will use these to construct some frameworks for professional observation and assessment.

1 Silvia is ten years old and attends residential special education. She has a speech impediment and behavioural learning difficulties. She returns from home one weekend, with bruising around her thighs and buttocks. The staff refer to social services, and a medical examination reveals that she has been frequently buggered. The perpetrator is her seventeen-year-old brother. Silvia persistently denies that she has been sexually abused, but she eventually breaks down and admits that it was her brother.

Table 6.2 The family and social context of the abuse (Silvia): assessing the family and social context of the abuse through the professional's observations of the child's physical, emotional, psychological, social and educational life

	Social Worker	*Health visitor*
Physical	Lack of co-ordination in mobility, less alert and cheerful in recent weeks. More tense. Very poor standard of hygiene in the home generally which causes child's own standards to fall when she's at home.	Poor standard of post-natal care recorded for all children in family. Very poor hygiene standards, affecting all the children.
Emotional	Very limited range of emotional responses. Seldom happy, smiling, curious or enthusiastic. Far more often sad and withdrawn.	
Psychological	Appears increasingly apprehensive and tension laden; seems to be ignored or isolated by family members. Her slow responses to mother's request for help is interpreted as defiance and leads to verbal assaults upon her.	
Social	Virtually no social life with family members, nor with children in the neighbourhood. She does not belong to any social/hobbies/sports clubs at home. Her speech impediment is mocked by siblings.	
Educational	Family contributes virtually nothing to child's educational achievements and development. This child doesn't expect anybody in the home to be excited about what she's made or done in school.	HV recalls that children, including Silvia, were often allowed, encouraged to miss school, with Silvia's 'special' problems being made the excuse.

GP	Paediatrician	Teacher	Other
Not a particularly healthy child by any means. Intermittent visits by Silvia and her mother. Bed wetting once a big problem.	Evidence of anal abuse. Also numerous bruises, possibly associated with anal abuse.	Child's physical activities in classroom and in sport have never been a matter of concern. But she has been returning each Monday recently, looking poorly, unslept and more unkempt than usual.	
'a pathetic little thing'.			
Appears easily frightened in surgery. Clings to mother, and screams. Mother tells her 'stop that nonsense'.			
		Speech impediment seriously limits her socializing potential. She does have friendships which she values, but these friends are similarly shy, unassertive, like herself.	
	Various psychological/ negative testing indicates that child's poor performances and responses stem from an apparent fear and tension, as much as they may do from her speech impediment and social and economic deprivation.	Child performs reasonably well in school. Responds particularly well to individual attention. Prefers to work close than in groups.	

Table 6.3   The family and social context of the abuse (Patricia): assessing the family and social context of the abuse through the professional's observation of the child's physical, emotional, psychological and social and educational life

	Social worker	*GP*
Physical	An attractive, confident, articulate girl. She interacts with her family and social worker in an impressive way.	Excellent health.
Emotional	She exhibits a wide range of emotional responses, humour, laughter, frustration, irritation, joy, anger, etc. She can be unshakeably stubborn too.	
Psychological	There is no indication of any psychological impairment. She seems confidently to grasp the meaning and influences of her own role in the family and of other family members. These roles are clearly defined and mutually respected or, at least, tolerated.	
Social	An active and successful social life; member of clubs; excellent swimmer; member of school's hockey and badminton teams.	
Educational	Educational, sports and hobbies, achievements, prominently displayed around the living room.	

Police	Teacher	Pastoral teacher	Other
Police remark on her self-confidence and determination when being interviewed.	Very high standard of personal hygiene; resents poor hygiene in other pupils. Excellent performance in school sports. Motivates others. Most often bright-eyed, alert and attentive.	Never had any need to counsel Patricia on physical/sexual matters.	
Police remark on her anger in response to their persistent questioning.	Agrees with social worker's observations.	Her emotional life seems very normal.	
Do not accept her denial. Believe that she is under strong pressure within herself, or from her father, to deny.	Teachers have not been aware of any psychological or other kind of pressures; her work has been consistently good. She is a clear thinker.		
	Popular and sociable in and out of class. Mixes mostly with high performers.	She is an active and well liked participant in the schools community enterprises/ charitable works.	
	Work indicates intelligence, and constant interests and support from parents. She will do well in exams.		

She begs people 'not to tell him that she has told'. Silvia's parents have recently separated. Her mother has had recurring mental health problems. There are two other children in the home, aged fourteen and eight. The family endure chronic poverty and are a constant source of concern to numerous statutory and voluntary agencies.

2　Patricia is a fifteen-year-old who has been repeatedly sexually abused by her father. There are two younger children, Peter, aged two, and Maureen, aged eight. The sexual abuse has occurred over a long period of time, beginning with what seemed entirely innocent embraces and kisses. It graduated to sexual intercourse, through masturbation and oral sex. Patricia told a close friend her secret, not out of any misery or pain, but actually telling her friend how enjoyable it was. Her friend didn't keep the secret. Patricia is approached by a teacher and denies what she told. Her father denies it too. Mother supports both of them. A medical examination is refused.

Let us look now at how the various professionals may observe each of these victims in their physical, emotional, psychological, social and educational functioning.

The implications of differences in social and family contexts

The only common factor in these cases is that a serious crime has been committed in each one. They differ sharply in every other significant respect. In the case of Silvia a child is crying out for rescue not just from the brutal sexual abuse perpetrated against her, but also, from the poverty, psychological cruelty and social degradations which abound in her family life. In the case of Patricia the child and family alike are telling social workers and police to naff off! They may in effect be saying that 'we don't need you' or 'that we are functioning well without you, thank you very much, and that if you impose yourselves upon us, you will make our lives a misery and destroy our family.' (This is not an uncommon utterance by teenage incest victims in particular, who know from instinct and from what they read that intervention 'to protect' in their particular case would be disastrous.) The knowledge that the family is already immersed in sexual abuse, and in the lies, self-deceptions, pervasive secrecy and general corruption which sustains that abuse, should not encourage professionals to ignore the family's resentment and hostility. The above observations of Patricia indicate that, in addition to these evils and their inevitable long-term effects, her family have nevertheless provided something else which she, more than anyone else, appreciates. It is difficult to accept this contradiction. It is, alas, a fact. Whereas Silvia's case warrants an immediate and massive intervention, social services and police would ignore Patricia's and her family's wishes at *the child's peril*. In respect of categorization, one can now see that Silvia's ghastly existence of brutal and sexual degradation does *not* make it a more serious case; on the contrary, it is relatively simple to rescue her and protect her, and to offer her a quality of care much superior to that which she has received. Patricia's case is infinitely more complex and dangerous and, where complexity and dangerousness are criteria for categorizing, this case must be near the top of the list. Ironically, in respect of priority of action – unless social workers and police officers know exactly what they are doing and the effects of each of their actions – the case of Patricia can safely go to the bottom of the list: this is one case where a lack of knowledge, experience, skills and technique on the part of any professionals who may become involved will fully justify leaving it alone. There are too many corpses lying around in the child sexual-abuse field to think otherwise.

A diagrammatic framework for categorizing the resources context

The resources context of child sexual abuse requires two separate diagrammatic frameworks, one for the resources of the agencies involved, and one for the resources of the individual worker at the front line. In the following tables, most of the case samples we have been using are included, and some of the particular problems arising within each one are highlighted. Enquiries about agency resources for coping with these problems revolve around the issues of categorization, child sexual-abuse specialization, leadership, philosophy, theory, quality of management, availability of practical facilities and therapeutic aids, and the training and expertise to use them, and, last but by no means least, the availability of alternative high-quality fostering and residential resources. Enquiries about professionals' resources revolve around the issues of training, principles and ethics, self-awareness, respect for and co-operation with other agencies, and assessment of risks and danger.

Summary and conclusions

The social-work profession can no longer pretend that it is obliged, willing and able to respond effectively to every single case of child sexual abuse brought to its attention. Social workers and social-services offices throughout the country have paid dearly in recent years as a consequence of that delusion. (So too have many other client groups which have been neglected in the post-'Childwatch' panic and preoccupation with child sexual abuse.) This chapter has attempted to grapple with the origins of that delusion, namely, the initial lack of awareness of the enormous diversity of child sexual-abuse cases and of the challenges that they pose for the numerous agencies and professionals. Literature and training for child sexual-abuse work has not yet seen fit to include the essential and systematic categorization of child sexual abuse. Consequently sweeping generalities of theory and practice have evolved from individual writers'/practitioners' very

Table 6.4　The resources of the agency in which you work

Cases: with particular problems encountered	Has your agency/ agencies categorized child sexual abuse, clearly identifying the greatest challenges within those categories and providing comprehensive guidelines and strategies for meeting those challenges?	Does your agency have or is it part of a multi-disciplinary child sexual-abuse team? Are the members specially trained, qualified and experienced in child sexual-abuse work? Is the leader in particular trained in this respect?	Does your team, agency and agencies share a particular philosophy of approach to child sexual abuse? Does it share any particular theoretical analysis of the causes of different types of child sexual abuse?
Sarah, 6½, allegedly abused by father (Ch. 1). Mother and father unite against agencies. Children are removed.			
Paul, 10, sexually abused by his mother, a single parent (Ch. 5). Paul is an only child and attends special school.			
Mary, 5, sexually abused by a male child-minder (Ch. 5). Both parents disgusted and angry.			
Joanne, 12, sexually abused by her stepfather (Ch. 6). Mother tells GP but doesn't want police or social services to know.			
Martin, 15, sexually abused by his mother; incestuous and symbiotic relationship (Ch. 6). Both mother and son deteriorate rapidly during enforced separation.			
Silvia, 10, sexually abused by 17-year-old brother (Ch. 6). Attends residential school weekdays. Chronic poverty in family. 2 younger children.			
Patricia, 15, sexually abused by father (Ch. 6). Doesn't want any agency to know or to interfere. Parents and child unite against agencies.			

Has management evolved policies based upon sound professional principles and practice, or has it repeatedly issued ill-thought-out, panicky policies and procedures in response to media or political pressures?

Does your agency or agencies combined provide adequate accommodation for interviewing victims, for access between victims and parent(s), for group work, play therapy, video recording? Does it provide all the necessary equipment for this? Are the staff/team members specially trained and experienced in using these facilities, i.e. group work, family therapy, engaging and working with perpetrators?

Is there adequate alternative accommodation?
1 *Fostering; foster parents trained and experienced in providing for sexually abused children?*
2 *Residential; staff trained and experienced for the same?*

Table 6.5   The individual professional's resources

Cases: with particular problems encountered	Are you trained, experienced or skilled in working with any particular category of child sexual abuse or any particular aspect of child sexual-abuse cases?	Do you have a clearly defined set of principles and a code of ethics for guiding you through complex and dangerous problem areas in child sexual-abuse work?
Sarah, 6½, allegedly abused by father (Ch. 1). Mother and father unite against agencies. Children are removed.		
Paul, 10, sexually abused by his mother, a single parent (Ch. 5). Paul is an only child and attends special school.		
Mary, 5, sexually abused by a male child-minder (Ch. 5). Both parents disgusted and angry.		
Joanne, 12, sexually abused by her stepfather (Ch. 6). Mother tells GP but doesn't want police or social services to know.		
Martin, 15, sexually abused by his mother; incestuous and symbiotic relationship (Ch. 6). Both mother and son deteriorate rapidly during enforced separation.		
Silvia, 10, sexually abused by 17-year-old brother (Ch. 6). Attends residential school weekdays. Chronic poverty in family. 2 younger children.		
Patricia, 15, sexually abused by father (Ch. 6). Doesn't want any agency to know or to interfere. Parents and child unite against agencies.		

Are you aware of precisely what it is in any of these cases which poses the greatest challenge to you, and why? Do you normally work within the guidelines of a social work categorization of child sexual abuse?

Are you respectful of other professionals' and other agencies' differing perceptions, attitudes and approach to child sexual abuse? Can you easily co-operate with these professionals?

Are you capable of weighing up all the risks involved in any proposed course of action, e.g. removal of child; allowing child to remain; removing siblings of child; permitting/denying access, etc.?

narrow experiences and have been vigorously applied to every type of child sexual-abuse act in every conceivable context in which such acts are committed.

The first task for social services is to differentiate between cases in which they have a statutory responsibility to intervene, and those in which they have neither responsibility nor right. There can be little doubt that the panic and hysteria generated in 1986–7 by well-meaning public figures and pressure groups wanting to help sexually abused children has led to the most serious and widespread assault upon the dignity and rights of many innocent and loving parents. Social workers have no moral, professional or legal right to intervene in child sexual abuse where it is clear that the parents have had no part to play in the abuse, are disgusted and angered by it, show sympathy, love and protection towards the victim and commit themselves to ensuring their child has no further contact with the perpetrator. Social workers have not just the right but the duty to intervene when the perpetrator (alleged or proven) is a parent or permanent carer of the child.

There are three major thrusts of enquiry to be made in attempting to categorize and prioritize child sexual-abuse cases. These revolve around the issues of protection, the family and social context of the abuse and the resources of the agency and individual professional(s) assigned to the case. There is one particular category of abuse in which enquiries about protection are critically important; these are certain types of incest cases, in which exposure may be perceived by the perpetrator or victim to be too threatening, and in which death, murder, suicidal pacts, etc., may be felt to be the only alternative. This is the most challenging and dangerous type of case and raises essential questions about the agencies' and the professionals' resources for coping. Resources often determine the size and nature of the challenges which particular categories of cases pose and, therefore, have to be scrutinized with as much rigour and discipline as is applied in assessing the 'protection' and the 'family and social context' issues.

Some diagrammatical frameworks have been provided. These may help in the task of categorizing and prioritizing. There can be no universally applied categorization or prioritization. The specific acts of abuse, the family and social contexts and the resources of agencies and professionals who have to deal with it will all vary enormously. Each social-services department, and possibly each division or area within the department, can embark upon its own categorizing, within the frameworks provided (or whatever other framework may be available).

7

The perpetrators of child sexual abuse

Introduction

During a recent two-day international conference (in Leeds, July 1988) on child sexual abuse, two of the workshops had to be cancelled because of an apparent lack of interest. The subject: perpetrators. Finkelhor (1986) states that 'perpetrators' are probably the most important and the most neglected area of study in child sexual abuse. From a social-work point of view their importance stems from the fact that their actions and influence both before and after the disclosure of their deeds can both sabotage or complement professional interventions on behalf of the child. This chapter, therefore, is based upon a practitioner's conviction that it is of paramount importance for social workers in particular to learn about certain types of perpetrators. It will begin with a general statement on the challenge which perpetrators pose. Then it will explore the 'gender' issue, i.e. the fact that child sexual abusers are predominently male, and their victims are predominantly female. What are the implications for social workers (particularly those specializing in child sexual-abuse work), the vast majority of whom are female?

This chapter will suggest that the sexual revolution of the 1960s may have significantly increased the number of child sexual-abuse perpetrators today. A detailed explanation underpinning this suggestion will be given. It is an explanation which lends support to the feminist analysis of sexual abuse as an expression of male power; the explanation itself is given some credence by frequent and consistent findings in the limited amount of research and writings on perpetrators. Probably one of the most common and challenging types of perpetrator is that of father/stepfather sexually abusing their daughters. Some recent research on this matter will be examined, as it casts serious doubts upon the more extreme feminist view that *all* men are potential sexual abusers of their own children.

One of the reasons why the topic of perpetrators provokes some anxiety, and why professionals generally want neither to engage nor learn about them, is because of an all-embracing perception shared by public and professionals alike: 'perpetrators' invariably conjures images of brutal monsters inflicting the most diabolical abuse upon innocent, defenceless, very young children. Of course, there are many instances of monstrous abuses, but there are also very many more different types of perpetrators abusing children of all ages through many different forms of abuse. A major task therefore, is to identify some aspects of the topic of perpetrators which are most relevant to social workers. This includes the enquiries: which perpetrators are social workers likely to encounter most? when are social workers most likely to encounter them? what sexual abuses do perpetrators most commonly commit? how precisely can social workers influence events for better or worse after disclosure? Within this examination lies the potential for social workers to be able to predict the degree and nature of influence which a perpetrator may have on a particular case, and to minimize or maximize that influence if it is in the child's best interests to do so. Some guidelines will be provided, and some of the pitfalls highlighted. Case examples will be frequently used to illustrate important points.

Perpetrators: the challenge for professionals

One of the reasons why writers, researchers and practitioners have given so little attention to the subject of perpetrators is because of ignorance of the enormous influence they may wield over victim, family and agency interventions. Professionals have often been perplexed and frustrated by victims' loyalties to the perpetrator and the complications this creates in the post-intervention period. In the child sexual-abuse hysteria of recent years, many professionals succumbed to the public view that, if children could be merely rescued from the abuse and perpetrators merely punished, the problem would be eradicated. Because of the difficulties that professionals themselves have in working with perpetrators, many *hoped* that this would be the case.

Police officers, social workers, probation and prison officers are more likely to have to work with perpetrators in varying degrees, at different times, than other professional groups. Social workers, however, are the only professionals who are likely to become involved with perpetrators and remain involved, from the time of disclosure and protection of the child, through investigation, prosecution and conviction; they are also likely to be involved if a released ex-perpetrator resides with children. This is not to suggest that the social-work role is more important or demanding; indeed, the actual contact they may have with perpetrators may be only a fraction of the time which, for example, probation and/or prison officers spend with perpetrators. But the social worker's role and relationship with perpetrators are unique nonetheless, not because of any responsibility the former may have for the latter, but because of the latter's ability to make life hellishly difficult for the former. It is the perpetrator's power and influence over the social worker's central (and statutory) goal of securing the welfare of the child, ensuring his or her continuous physical, emotional and psychological good health, which determines the importance of this abysmally neglected area of child sexual-abuse work.

The gender factor: the lessons from physical abuse

Most police officers have no difficulty at all in 'working with' perpetrators. They simply aim to lock them up. Most police officers are male, and in virtually every case of apprehending, interrogating and prosecuting a perpetrator there will be a male officer involved. Most social workers are female. Social workers generally do find difficulty in engaging perpetrators of child sexual abuse, but female social workers may have even greater difficulty. They may believe that there is no role for social workers; they may be guided by a philosophy (e.g. some strands of feminist thinking) which dictates that the only response should be a severe judicial, punitive one; or they may have personal and very painful memories of being sexually abused themselves, which would make it almost impossible for them to work effectively or objectively with perpetrators. Some male social workers too may share all these possible reasons for avoiding perpetrators.

Perpetrators of child sexual abuse, however, should not be seen as presenting some unique, insurmountable challenge to social workers. Similar difficulties have been experienced in the recent history of physical abuse. Child abuse inquiries (Beckford, Colwell, Henry, etc.) invariably demonstrate the marked reluctance of professionals even to have contact with the perpetrators. The consequences have always been disastrous in those cases. The excuse given, namely, that the male perpetrator was never at home, was at work, was working late, etc., was hardly convincing. The real reason was that professional, mostly middle-class, mostly female social workers, had not the slightest inclination to engage male perpetrators whom they perceived as violent or threatening, incomprehensible or beyond the pale. They were content (and relieved) to continue visiting mother week after week, and to be making the most wildly optimistic assessments on the basis of those visits. Fourteen years separate the Colwell and the Beckford tragedies. The failure of social workers to engage the perpetrator was a major feature in both cases. These were no exceptions to the rule, no mere aberration of professional practice; on the contrary, they are symptomatic of a pervasive vulnerability in professionals as a whole. Mother is always the easy option for professionals, female professionals in particular; she is more accommodating, willing to listen, least resistant to the professionals' suggestions, particularly when the perpetrator isn't there. There is, however, a consequence of this vulnerability which is most pertinent to the current analysis of the causes of child sexual abuse. As we have seen, the family-therapy perspective emphasizes 'mother's responsibility' in many abuse cases, either through her failure to protect the child, or by colluding in knowing or suspecting that the abuse is happening, but not taking the appropriate action. The professional's tendency to avoid male perpetrators (of both physical and sexual abuse), and to depend solely upon establishing a good relationship and plenty of regular contact with the mother, actually invests her with a power and authority more apparent than real. Professionals often regard and treat the mother as if she *does* have this power and authority, a delusion that reassures them that mother will be able to protect the child. This misperception is really a defence on the part of professionals unable to use their own very real power and authority to engage and to exert some control over perpetrators. The consequence of this, of course, is that mother is more likely to be blamed if something does go wrong. There is surely no greater hypocrisy (and ironic cruelty towards a mother) than to exploit her in this way, using her to avoid the principal and often the only source of risk to the child, namely the male perpetrator, thereby unwittingly exposing her to vilification and persecution when she is unable to protect the child from that same perpetrator.

This may be difficult for social workers to accept. It does, however, highlight a serious failing in social-work literature and training generally, and in child sexual-abuse training and literature in particular. There is still no effective, tested, self-awareness training available for social workers in this country (O'Hagan 1986a, 1986b). True, there is increasingly a self-awareness component in training for child sexual-abuse work (Metropolitan Police and Bexley, 1987) but that invariably concentrates only upon the impact of the particular deeds of perpetrators, i.e. a concentration upon specific child sexual-abuse acts. Social workers do not need insight into why particular acts of abuse repel or horrify them; even less do they need to be invited to imagine themselves as victims being subjected to the most degrading and traumatic kind of abuse (it is insulting to the real victims of sexual abuse for professionals to pretend that they can replicate ghastly experiences in this way). What social workers do need is the most rigorous and honest self-exploration of their own vulnerabilities when they encounter perpetrators; to realize how that vulnerability can minimize their effectiveness in serving the victim. 'Gender vulnerability' is a major problem for social workers, male and female, whether it be the vulnerability of men or women reluctant or frightened to engage male perpetrators of child abuse generally, or the reluctance or fear of female social workers to engage child sexual-abuse perpetrators in particular.

Explanation and theory

The sixties connection

In Thatcherite Britain the view that the permissive sixties were some kind of lunatic aberration is not uncommon. Consequently there is much rejoicing

today in the belief that nearly every manifestation of the pervasive
philosophy and revolutionary fervour of the sixties, particularly that
pertaining to social welfare and personal freedom, has been thoroughly
discredited. Be that as it may, there are numerous 'gains' and 'achievements'
of the 1960s which are still tenaciously guarded. The most obvious of these
remains sexual freedom. No doubt, some will shout 'AIDS' as proof that the
sexual revolution of the sixties has also been turned on its head; but any
consideration of the existing literature and advice about AIDS will clearly
demonstrate that the freedoms enshrined in that revolution are as popular
and as sought after today as they were then. They espouse the right of
individuals to explore sexual curiosity and pursue sexual fulfilment in
whatever way they may choose. AIDS has done little to challenge this
conviction; it has merely necessitated the recommendation to use condoms
in exercising those rights.

Sexual freedom and child sexual abuse

Neither the advocates nor the few opponents of the sexual liberation of the
1960s had any reason to consider whether or not it increased the risk of
children being sexually abused. After all, there was neither official nor
public recognition of such abuse in those flower-power-loving days. The
suggestion (let alone the reality) that thousands of individual adults may
have been engaging in what was perceived to be the worst kind of abuse of
their own children (which we now know they were) simply would not have
been taken seriously. Yet 'permissiveness' carried on in its own merry way,
advocating as much sexual experimentation and gratification as one wanted,
and propagating the view that individuals were unfulfilled in proportion to
their reluctance or failure to do so. Permissiveness was supported and
intensified by an avalanche of increasingly explicit verbal, photographic and
cinematic pornography, which enhanced the status of sexual exploits in
day-to-day conversations and interactions within many peer groups. Sexual
encounters and sexual experimentation became a kind of societal premium,
relegating chastity and marital fidelity to the scrap heap of a bygone
best-forgotten age. In the latter was perceived the causes of misery,
oppression and insanity.
   Although the prevailing climate of permissiveness enabled parliament to
liberalize the laws on homosexuality, and facilitated the emergence of a
number of paedophile organizations (the two developments not necessarily
related), it should be stressed that the sexual revolution focused upon
'conventional' heterosexual relationships. Sexual gratification and sexual
prowess were sought and encouraged primarily in respect of adult female/
male relationships, couples of a similar age, intelligence and social scale.
There was, however, a category of persons who, despite all the 'literary',
cinematic and sex educative aids, were destined to remain on the periphery
of the sexual revolution. They might have been titillated like many were by

the novelty of pornographic literature and films, but they were to remain incapable of satisfying any consequential sexual appetite in the 'conventional' male/female sexual relationship way. These were socially inadequate people, people who have difficulty integrating within their own peer groups, who cannot easily communicate with or relate to the opposite sex, commonly perceived as miserable and pathetic, immature, too serious or too tense. They were not unique to the sixties. They exist in all eras, in every culture. Generally, they are tolerated, sometimes pitied, but when they attempt to engage in any kind of intimacy – particularly sexual intimacy of the kind so vigorously propagated in the sixties – they are likely to be rejected and humiliated.

It is precisely this kind of male perpetrator, socially inadequate and pathetic, who has been consistently identified by writers and researchers. Berliner and Stevens (1982: 99) speak of them as 'characteristically self centred, immature and insecure . . . who have difficulty with interpersonal relationships . . .'. Chandler (1982: 60) talks about the 'emotionally unstable father, paranoid, insecure about his own masculinity . . .'. Conte (1982: 7) notes the perpetrator's 'overpowering feelings of inadequacy, dependency, and anxiety . . . which becomes disguised as genital urges . . . directed towards those . . . least capable of retaliation . . .'. Furniss (1983: 267) speaks of a common basic pattern of sexually abusing fathers who are 'weak, sexually frustrated, demanding, emotionally immature and dependent . . .'. Sgroi (1982b: 127) labels them as 'Me first' individuals, who 'satisfy many non sexual needs when engaging in sexual behaviour . . .' (i.e. sexually abusing children). In a perpetrator's case history, Wyre (1987: 10) begins:

> Ronald was easily abused and bullied in school, where he was regarded as a wimp and a loner. He was spotty and felt unattractive. He was unassertive, and lacked any sense of purpose. He had bed wetting problems, felt rejected, and in adolescence found it impossible to get girlfriends.

Wyre has recently produced a training package for working with perpetrators (1987). It contains the most comprehensive and systematic profiles of nearly all sexual abusers generally. In its categorization of child sexual-abuse perpetrators, it repeatedly highlights such characteristics as 'underdeveloped peer relationships, poor quality of life style, may be seen as the social misfit, withdrawn, has the problem of dealing with sexuality when unable to form relationships, is lonely and isolated, etc.'

Finally, in Giarretto's observation (1981: 188), we may be seeing the likely outcome for Wyre's client Ronald:

> stewing in a state of chronic resentment which can be discharged only through hostile acts, unconsciously intended to be self punishing . . . reinforcing and discharging his low self worth . . . he approaches his child sexually, without full awareness of the needs drives and motives

fuelling his behaviour, nor of its consequences to his child, family and himself. . . .

The power factor

Whatever the limitations and flaws in the research and writing on perpetrators (commented upon by Finkelhor (1986)), social workers in Britain are daily making these same observations of perpetrators. I have not yet encountered a perpetrator without some of the above inadequacy characteristics which, as nearly all social workers can testify, are exacerbated by the severe environmental and economic deprivations in which many of these perpetrators live. To return to the sixties, we should now ask what was the impact of the sexual revolution, with all its propaganda about fulfilment and 'self-actualization' etc., supposedly achieved through sexual exploration and gratification with one's partner(s) of the opposite sex – what was its impact upon those inadequate, socially isolated individuals who had inherent difficulties in achieving single partner intimacy of any kind? To have one's sexual curiosity and feelings continually aroused by the permissive propaganda of the day, and never to be able to gratify that curiosity and sexual desire in the way that was repeatedly illustrated, must have greatly magnified the individual's sense of inadequacy, frustration, envy and sexual powerlessness. It must also have caused them to contemplate alternatives and to look elsewhere. It is the sense of powerlessness which is the most potent force in motivating and directing such individuals towards a type of victim over whom they could easily exercise power and, at the same time, sexually gratify themselves as much as everyone was then being urged to do. The more isolation and rejection these perpetators might endure at the hands of their peer groups, then the greater their need sexually to abuse those who are even more powerless than themselves, and the more gratifying too. The stark innocence and vulnerability of children, their inability to protest or resist, made them and still makes them particularly attractive to these inadequates.

It is significant that the recent exposure of child sexual abuse has allegedly been made on the basis of thousands of research respondents' present-day memories of sexual abuse perpetrated against them in and around the sixties. No one has, as yet, asked: why the sixties? On the contrary, it has been assumed that, if adults of any age had been involved in similar research, they would have provided the same answers. Thus today's research on adults who reveal the extent of child sexual abuse perpetrated against them in the sixties dubiously concludes that the same problem must have existed *to the same extent* at other times. There is not the slightest justification for believing this to be the case. Today, despite the widespread Thatcherite contempt for the sixties, and the Thatcherite successes in reversing many of the trends of the sixties, the problem addressed in the above theoretical explanation has not only been untouched, it has actually got worse. It has got worse because those identified, socially inadequate, prospective child sexual abusers, are now one of the principal target groups of a pornography industry which has expanded to alarming proportions. It now produces a type of pornography that, in its perversion, violence and illegality, is well beyond the imagination of the most enthusiastic advocates of permissiveness in the sixties. The black-market pornographic video industry, with its sizeable child sexual-abuse component, is thriving (Ennew 1986), despite Thatcherism. Does anyone seriously believe that this kind of material does *not* influence the type of prospective perpetrator who has been repeatedly and unanimously identified? Can there be any doubt that it motivates him all the more to seek sexual gratification and power by sexually abusing vulnerable children?

Two final points ought to be made on this matter. First, there probably are other categories of perpetrators and prospective perpetrators of child sexual abuse. In recent months we have read of apparently sane, sensible and highly successful professional men who have been exposed as perpetrators. They are not pathetic, socially inadequate individuals. But their numbers are so small in comparison with the others (small perhaps, only in respect of the number who have been caught), that they do not as yet constitute a category of perpetrators whose characteristics are identifiable. Second, the above theoretical suggestion does not seek to explain the causes of child sexual abuse. It merely focuses upon certain historical factors and observable characteristics of known perpetrators which would explain the probable dramatic increase in the incidence of child sexual abuse.

The extreme feminist view

The suggestion that men's sexual abuse of children is a manifestation of man's pervasive and perpetual attempt to dominate women is central to the feminist perspective on child sexual abuse (see Chapter 3). There is a branch of feminism which, however, takes this theoretical generalization much further, propagating a view that *all* men are potential sexual abusers, *even of their own children*. Regrettably the hysteria and panic generated within social-services departments in recent years enabled this theory to become respectable and influential in social-work and feminist publications, and in the burgeoning child sexual-abuse literature and training. The most articulate expression of the theory is made by Glaser and Frosh (1988), in a text published only a few months before the Cleveland report itself was published. The timing is ironic, as Cleveland demonstrated the disastrous and inevitable consequences of a half-baked child sexual-abuse strategy clearly based upon extreme feminist views (naturally the only resources needed, if you believe that every man is a potential child sexual abuser, even of his own child, is a pocketful of place-of-safety orders!).

Glaser and Frosh believe that men are 'emotionally illiterate', and that 'sex is one of the few socially acceptable ways in which men can aspire to (*emotional*) closeness with others'. As such, sex becomes 'the carrier of all the unexpressed desires that men's emotional illiteracy produces'. Men are conditioned to reject emotion, and their identities are based upon that rejection. Sex is and should be a very emotional act. Such men cannot tolerate that; they detach sex from emotion and limit it 'to the action of the penis, an act rather than an encounter' (p. 24). The origins of this condition of man lies in long-established socialization processes in which there is a striving for a 'masculinity which focuses on dominance and independence, an orientation to the world which is active and assertive, which valorizes competitiveness and turns its face from intimacy, achieving esteem in the glorification of force . . .' (p. 24).

It is not merely a limited category of potential abusers whom the authors have in mind in constructing this theory; in a later passage they make it clear that their theoretical man is the rule rather than the exception:

> there are systematic features of masculine sexuality which contribute to sexual abuse; in some ways, it is the inhibition which non abusive men demonstrate towards sex with children that has to be explained more than the acts of the others. . . .
>
> (pp. 25–6)

In Chapter 3 the feminist contribution to the whole field of child sexual abuse was given the recognition and status which it deserves. It is all the more regrettable, therefore, that during the period between 'Childwatch' and Cleveland, there was a glut of published extreme feminist views on child sexual abuse which received far more publicity (and mockery) than the original, valued contribution. These extreme views are damaging for a more important reason: they serve only to exacerbate reluctance and apprehensions felt by practitioners (those at least who might take the views and the theory seriously) about working with perpetrators. Furthermore, they contribute nothing towards the crucial task of enlisting the general public's support in combating child sexual abuse. Men can hardly be expected to take the problem seriously when self-appointed experts in child sexual abuse are telling them that men achieve their 'esteem in the glorification of force', and that every single one of them is a potential child sexual abuser.

Fortunately, there is research which actually addresses the question of which men abuse and which do not abuse in respect of a very common child sexual-abuse act, i.e. fathers/stepfathers sexually abusing their daughters. Parker and Parker (1986) sought to examine a number of theories explaining the aetiology of this type of abuse, the biosocial theory of incest avoidance, and Bowlby's theory on the nature of early parent/child bonding. They also tested out a number of hypotheses which have emerged from recent research (often elevated by the uncritical to something far more than mere hypotheses). What makes this research very impressive is a superior methodology and the use of a non-abusive comparison or control group, both of which have usually been absent from all previous research on perpetrators, a lack which rightly Finkelhor (1986) questions. Finkelhor's excellent analysis of all child sexual-abuse research was completed before the publication of this particular work. Its findings should be of particular interest to social workers.

⮱ Parker and Parker did not support the view that parental absences and parental discord in the early home situation are significant risk factors for the occurrence of the sexual abuse under study. Second, they did support the view that a father who was abused in his own childhood was more likely sexually to abuse his daughter than those who were not abused. Third, a father/stepfather's absence in the first three years of his daughter's life was a marked characteristic in the father–daughter sexually abusing situation. Finally, the most significant high-risk factor was when fathers/stepfathers played no part at all in child care and nurturant activities in the earliest years of their daughter's life.

Very few stepfathers play any part in the nursing, feeding and comforting of their stepchildren in the earliest years of their life, for the simple reason that stepfathers do not usually come on the scene until their stepchildren are well past infancy. We know – another one of the very rare unanimous views about anything in child sexual abuse – that stepfathers are far more likely sexually to abuse their stepchildren than are fathers likely to abuse their children. Parker and Parker seem to have found a very convincing reason for this, the implication being that a father's love of and commitment towards his new-born child, and, thereafter (particularly for the first three years), his sharing in the physical and emotional caring for that child, creates a powerful prohibition to sexually abusing that child in any way. Of even greater significance in this research is the clear indication that the family factor, i.e. whether or not the perpetrator is a relative of the child, usually meaning the father/stepfather, is of much less importance than the nature and quality of the relationship that exists between the infant child and the father or substitute father figure.

This rightly removes an unhelpful emphasis that has been placed upon 'family' in the child sexual-abuse debate, with the family-systems therapists and theorists arguing that the abuse stems from dysfunctional relationships and mother's collusion and responsibility, and the feminists arguing that, just as every man is a potential sexual abuser, so too every family has 'the ethos of privacy and possessiveness' which 'holds the seeds of sexual exploitation' (Glaser and Frosh 1988: 42). Just as the family-therapy emphasis upon 'collusion' and 'responsibility' can be offensive to women in general and mothers in particular, so too are these extremist views to men in general, and fathers in particular. Many of the latter have actually had the pleasure of fully sharing in the physical and emotional caring of their children from the day that those children were born, the reason why many of them are incapable of sexually abusing those children, and why any suggestion to the contrary is either a source of mockery or deep offence to them. Parker and Parker are in effect asking us to forget about the search for that all-embracing, most convenient theory, which will provide the analysis most compatible with our own ideological prejudices and feelings. They have produced research which should compel us to focus upon single, identifiable characteristics in each abusing situation, not for the purpose of supporting any all-embracing theory, but to enable us to construct frameworks in which crucial factors and variables (such as the hitherto totally neglected one of the degree of 'paternal deprivation') can be explored.

The general impact of these widely publicized extreme feminist views of perpetrators, and of the supposedly 'inherent potential evils of family life' has been an initial provocation, which has eventually resolved itself in scepticism or mockery. Thus the widespread approval of the Cleveland report, unfortunately perceived as vindicating all those (including the *Sun* the *Star* and the *Mail*) who believed that the incidence of child sexual abuse was grossly exaggerated and that the whole Cleveland tragedy was caused by a bunch of power-hungry, man-hating feminists, 'managed' by wimps and fools whom they trampled all over.

Establishing boundaries in pursuit of knowledge about perpetrators

The problem with any theory zealously guarded and rigidly applied to all the complex issues in child sexual abuse is that it will discourage one from discriminating, categorizing and prioritizing. Just as it is necessary for social workers to do this in respect of child sexual-abuse acts and the circumstances surrounding them, so too must they establish boundaries in their perceptions of and in their work with perpetrators.

Which perpetrators should social workers learn about, and what precisely should they learn about them? The answer to the first question is: those perpetrators whom they are likely to encounter most. We must establish then who they are, the offences they are likely to commit and when social workers are likely to come into contact with them. The answer to the second question is: we should learn about characteristics of differing types of perpetrators and acquire any knowledge that enables social workers to predict obstacles and challenges which the perpetrator may place in their way.

Who are they?
Social workers are not likely to encounter too many international pornographers of child sexual abuse, nor aggressive attacking sadistic sexually abusing strangers, nor dirty old men on street corners, in amusement arcades, public toilets and cinemas, etc. Social workers are, however, likely to encounter numerous sexually abusing stepfathers and fathers (or substitute stepfather/fathers), also uncles, brothers and male lodgers in the same household as the child victim; they may occasionally encounter sexually abusing mothers, sisters, grandfathers and neighbours. They will most certainly hear of, though not necessarily encounter, many teenage

baby-sitting child sexual abusers. The vast majority of these perpetrators will live in already fragmented families in the densely populated communities and sprawling council estates in which social workers spend most of their time. This is not to suggest that most child sexual abuse occurs amongst poverty-stricken fragmented families in sprawling council estates; it is merely stating the fact that the bulk of child sexual-abuse work done by social-services social workers is carried out in those same areas in which the vast majority of them are already working. Finally, perpetrators encountered by social workers are most unlikely to have developed any bonding in the earliest childhood years of their victims. (This conclusion of Parker and Parker is the most conspicuous feature of hundreds of perpetrators encountered by social workers in Leeds during the last four years.)

What sexual abuse offences do they perpetrate?
Every conceivable form of sexual abuse is perpetrated against children by these (mostly) male and related perpetrators (See list of abuses in table 6.1). There are no reliable research statistics to tell us which child sexual-abuse offences social workers encounter most, but my own experiences support the view of Finkelhor (1979) and Conte (1982), that sexual intercourse between the perpetrator and child is the exception rather than the rule. Manual and oral masturbation is a very common form of abuse encountered by social workers, as it is in child sexual abuse generally (Chandler 1982). (One must not however lose sight of the most horrific abuses which have come to light in recent years, e.g. the rape of a four-year-old girl by her father, whilst she was held down for that purpose by her mother; the rape and buggery of a three-year-old by her mother's cohabitee and his male companion; the murder of a six-year-old through a morphine overdose before engaging her in video-recorded intercourse.)

When does the social worker encounter the perpetrator?
Perpetrators may be encountered at any time, from the day they first offend, to the day that they leave prison for a string of offences. The time at which they are encountered can be crucial for the management of a case; those who are exposed or who are justifiably accused after a first offence are not likely to be able to resist clear evidence that they have abused; they will be too petrified. Those who have been abusing their own or related child for a long time may well have prepared for an attempted exposure and, unless the evidence against them is overwhelming, may succeed in resisting that attempt. Another problem with the latter type, particularly if a father, is that he is likely to have considerable influence within the family, if only out of the permanency of his place, his habits, his economic contribution, and of the image of stability he presents of himself and the family to the outside world. The continuation of that influence over a long period of time during which he is abusing his child, can only further strengthen his defences against exposure.

Social workers have no responsibilities for the welfare of convicted perpetrators when they are released from prison. This is normally the task of the probation service. But social workers may well encounter such a perpetrator at this time when they are involved in protecting other children (social services and other child-protection agencies have to be forewarned about these releases and informed when they actually take place, with particular reference to where the perpetrator intends to stay. The presence of such an offender in the same household as a child may justify removal of that child).

Let us now look at a particular case, and explore some of the neglected area of agency–perpetrator interactions, and the implications for intervention.

Family composition

MOTHER: Peggy, unemployed, aged twenty-nine
CHILDREN: Jackie, aged eleven
 Tom, allegedly abused child, aged nine
 Kevin, allegedly abused child, aged five
COHABITEE AND SUSPECTED PERPETRATOR: Peter, aged twenty-six
FATHER: Pat (living elsewhere) aged thirty-eight

Family history

Peggy has been cohabiting with Peter for about a year; her husband Pat left about six months previous to that. Peggy has custody of the three children; Pat has access. The access arrangements have never been adhered to; Jackie, the oldest child, has increasingly spent more time with her father; nobody has objected or done anything about it. Peggy, Peter and three children live in very old dilapidated terrace housing.

Their father Pat lives in another part of town but remains very 'interested' in what's going on. The children are a constant source of continuing friction, dispute and allegations about old and present times between the parents, each one emphasizing the other's inadequacy as a parent.

The referral

Tom, the middle child, attends a special school. The school nurse is not satisfied with his explanation for some bruising which she observes one day. He is brought to hospital and given a thorough examination, during which indications of anal abuse are found. The paediatrician thinks it may have been digital rather than penile penetration. Tom does not disclose that he was abused, but he appears to be frightened.

Mother is contacted alone and persuaded to allow the other two children to be examined. She is, however, angry that discussions and an investigation took place without her knowing. Kevin, the youngest child, appears to the paediatrician to have been sexually abused. He occasionally speaks of Peter hurting his bottom. He can give no further details, nor can he enlighten the paediatrician and social worker through the use of anatomical dolls. There are no indications of abuse to Jackie, the oldest child.

What we need to know about alleged perpetrators

All previous child sexual-abuse literature and training would focus entirely upon the ways and means of gaining a disclosure from either of these children and ensuring their protection from further abuse by the alleged perpetrator, at any cost. The perpetrator would have been seen as a problem for the police. A typical police response to the referral from social services would be for the police immediately to question Peter, yet nothing could be better calculated to make life difficult for the social worker(s), and for ensuring the worst possible intervention on behalf of the children. It is also highly unlikely to achieve the desired results of an admission. Much investigative groundwork on this perpetrator is necessary before anyone begins confronting him with the allegations that have been made against him. The information that is required falls into two separate categories: first, information that adds weight to whatever evidence or indicators one already has that he actually is the perpetrator, i.e. record of any crimes against children or known characteristics which easily fit into a particular perpetrator profile. For example, we already see that there has been no bonding whatsoever between him and the children. That is always the most significant factor, rather than the fact that he is not a family member. Nor is there any indication of an existing vital investment by him in the children's development; that can easily be tested out through interviewing him and the children together with mother. We should also attempt to find out about his general life style, what kind of social life he has, how many friends, male and female, how socially confident or lacking in confidence he is, the quality of his own upbringing, his schooling, his job or unemployment. Second, and probably more important, social workers should learn as much as they possibly can about the influence which this perpetrator can exert upon the mother of the children, and upon the ongoing, unfinished marital dispute between mother and the father he has replaced. They should also try to learn about the likely reaction of the father to the news that his replacement (Peter) is being accused by his child(ren) of sexually abusing them.

Predicting the influence of perpetrators

What is the point of such enquiries? Why shouldn't the police move as quickly as they usually do in apprehending and removing this alleged perpetrator? Why shouldn't social workers immediately carry out their statutory duty of protecting children from alleged sexual abuse? How could the police be expected to be either interested in or delayed by such enquiries?

These are questions which have not yet been properly addressed. It is surely advantageous to gain as much information as possible about the alleged perpetrator, particularly 'perpetrator indicators' if they exist, before actually launching into the task of gaining an admission; it must surely increase the confidence of social worker and police officer to know, for example, that the habits, life style, abuse in childhood, previous convictions, etc., of the alleged perpetrator clearly fit into a particular perpetrator category. The consequences of a lack of such initial enquiries in the past, replaced only by 'the lightning strike', have often been a confident denial by the alleged perpetrator, support for him by the mother, intensification of the conflict between mother and her former husband, utter confusion and suffering for the children (compounded if they are removed) and no evidence whatsoever for a prosecution and conviction.

Let's imagine that the perpetrator does indeed exert great influence over Peggy, the mother, and that Peggy's loyalty to him is partially generated by her ex-husband's increasing criticism of them both – a very common situation for social workers. Let's imagine that, when she is first approached about the allegation, one of her thoughts is how cockahoop her husband will now feel. Is it likely then that a police visit and the removal of Peter for questioning will enable her to co-operate with social workers and, more importantly, to think and to act purely, primarily, in the interests of protecting her children?

The need to isolate the perpetrator

Here is a mightily protected alleged perpetrator and, if police and social services go pounding in, the most likely consequence is that they will actually strengthen his protection even more. This alleged perpetrator needs to be isolated, not protected, and that means the most careful cautious strategy of approach to the children's mother and the declared exclusion of the children's father. It should exclusively be the social worker's task to make this approach to mother; to empathize with her first as to the enormous risks that the allegation of abuse has created for her. In this case a costly and common blunder has already been made: initial, justifiable suspicions of abuse were not shared with mother; and a decision to take the child to hospital from his special school was made without either her knowledge or her approval. That would have to be acknowledged to mother, and an apology made. Recognition and sympathy are necessary too in respect of the problems posed by her ex-husband; the fact that she has been left with the responsibility of coping with three children singlehandedly, only to be criticized and condemned by her husband at the slightest opportunity. When that broad-based empathic approach is made, the social worker can then attempt to explore whether or not mother can freely choose to co-operate and protect her children from an alleged abuser; whether or not she is capable of believing that he is an abuser (most often the insensitive and speedy intervention by police and social services convinces this kind of mother not just that her boyfriend is incapable of such abuse, but that both he and she are victims of both agencies and must therefore support each other to the hilt); and whether or not she can facilitate and reconcile herself to the alleged perpetrator's removal. So often social workers will reply in the negative to all of these enquiries, i.e. that mother chooses *not* to protect her children; that she cannot believe her boyfriend *could be* a perpetrator, and that she *cannot* live without him. As has been made clear in chapter 5, and fully illustrated in chapter 1, such reactions from mother are provoked far more by poor agency intervention, which actually hurts and threatens mother most, than by any inherent irresponsibility on her part. It is often professionals' lack of knowledge and planning, their needless helplessness in knowing what to do about the perpetrator, which causes them to offend mothers in this way.

The ex-perpetrator

One of the consequences of the exposure of child sexual abuse in recent years has been the conviction and imprisonment of hundreds of perpetrators. Already social-services departments are having to face up to an additional and fastest growing category of perpetrator, namely those (mostly male) perpetrators released on parole or freed altogether. Apart from its being the fastest-growing category, experience tells us that it is the most problematic and dangerous category, with the risk of reoffending very high. Ex-perpetrators face a daunting task; they are labelled for life; many of them have had to remain in solitary confinement for their own protection; they are disowned by family and friends, shunned by society, and often feel that they are harassed by police and social workers. Despite the commitment and effort of probation officers, their eventual destination is often the doss house or the hostel. Though not always.

Here again, one has to rely on one's own and one's colleagues' experiences. Child sexual-abuse literature and training is not yet aware of the problem. The problem is that there are many single mothers with small children, whose lives are so miserable, who have experienced nothing but poverty and degradation and brutality (including sexual abuse itself), who are already dependent upon and subject to intrusive monitoring by all the child-care agencies, who can see no prospect of a better life, and who therefore are vulnerable to the overtures made by even the most pathetic and despised men they are likely to meet. Such perpetrators are again to be found in the sprawling council estates already so familiar to social workers. There they may integrate well, losing themselves in the chaos and family fragmentation all around. These men and these conditions constitute a terrible menace to children already blighted by the long-term poverty and deprivation of their mothers, and the environmental decay of their localities.

That gender factor again

In the case previously discussed, the strategy of approach for dealing with the alleged perpetrator revolved around establishing the right relationship and an empathy with mother. In some ways that may have been less challenging than any direct approach to the alleged perpetrator. In the case of a released offender, there may well be no time for such strategies, nor is there any moral justification for depending upon mother to make the right decision. Obviously the age, sophistication and intelligence of the children in the household are a crucial factor; the younger and the more vulnerable (special needs, handicap, etc?), then the greater the danger. The older the children, then the more justification for considering their capacity for protecting themselves, particularly if, for example, they are strong-willed adolescents who have taken a liking to their new lodger and were joining in the 'naff off' chorus towards the social worker. The ex-perpetrator must be confronted by the social worker, albeit with the cautionary protection of a police officer at his or her side. He should be told bluntly the facts of how often perpetrators reoffend, of the department's right – should it decide to enforce it – of removing children whom it thinks are in danger of being sexually abused; of why the department believes the multiple problems of the mother may have made her less protective than she would expect herself to be; and of the department's determination to take over that protective function, whatever the opposition from either the perpetrator or the mother.

This is no easy task for social workers (nor for their manager either). In our previous look at the gender factor (pp. 93–4), we discussed the difficulties that perpetrators in general posed to female social workers in particular; here we are dealing with a specific category of perpetrator – convicted, imprisoned with other perpetrators, most likely hardened rather than cured – who will pose major challenges to *any* social worker. Social workers really do detest having to meet, let alone confront, such men. Here then is the case of greatest temptation for the social worker to indulge in that most common tendency of avoiding the perpetrator, and hoping (beyond hope) that the already over-burdened mother can bail them out from such an awful task. It is not just being apprehensive of confronting men like these that makes the task so difficult; there are also the qualms which social workers might have if they perceive the task as nothing more than the hounding of a man who has already endured some kind of living hell for the offence he has committed. I can recall a number of occasions when ex-perpetrators looked me straight in the eye, and asked me: 'Do I have to be hounded like this for the rest of my life?' In the vast majority of cases there are neither the resources nor the willingness to consider any alternative that might just enable one to answer 'No'.

Summary and conclusions

The difficult and complex challenges of seeking out those children who are being sexually abused, enabling them to disclose what has happened to them, and thereafter ensuring their protection, have preoccupied writers, researchers and practitioners to the extent that they have been unable to give any time at all to the equally complex and difficult issue of child sexual-abuse perpetrators. Social workers in particular have felt exposed and vulnerable in working with alleged and proven perpetrators, because of the latter's potential for sabotaging the efforts of the former. There is a 'gender' issue for social workers who have to make contact with perpetrators. Male child abusers generally present formidable difficulties to social workers; male child sexual abusers are particularly challenging for female social workers. There is an unspoken history of social workers having too many unrealistic expectations and hopes that mothers can protect children; the reason stems more from an avoidance of the male perpetrator than a genuine conviction that mother really can protect.

The pornography and permissiveness of the sixties may have increased the number of perpetrators substantially. Perpetrators have been invariably identified as weak, inadequate, friendless individuals who have great difficulty in achieving satisfactory peer group (social and sexual) relationships. The sixties heralded an era in which much importance was attached to sexual freedom and experimentation. For those unable to achieve normal healthy social interactions, let alone sexual intercourse with the opposite sex, the consequence of ceaseless permissiveness propaganda could only be to intensify their sense of inadequacy and sexual frustration. Vulnerable children provided a ready-made answer, gratifying their sexual appetite, and imbuing them with a sense of power which they were otherwise incapable of achieving.

Recent impressive research has demonstrated that 'paternal deprivation' is a conspicuous feature in father–daughter incest. The same research shows that, when fathers are actively involved in the caring and nurturing of their children in the earliest years, this creates a powerful prohibition to the sexual abuse of those children. This research casts serious doubts over the validity of many extreme feminist views, particularly that which believes that *all* men are capable of sexually abusing their own children.

Like most other issues in child sexual abuse, 'perpetrators' lacks a systematic categorization and framework specifically relevant to social workers. Some attempt has been made in this chapter to focus on the questions of who are the perpetrators social workers most often encounter, when are they most likely to be encountered and which type of offence are they most likely to commit.

The most fundamental flaw in the training of social workers working with child sexual abuse is the total ignoring of the task of how to isolate perpetrators and minimize their influence when they have integrated themselves and achieved considerable influence in vulnerable fragmented families. Interventions invariably fail as a consequence. The task may be even more difficult if the perpetrator has returned from prison and been accepted gladly by a mother. If her children are particularly young and vulnerable, social workers must confront that perpetrator and seek his voluntary removal. If he refuses to move and if the mother supports him, then consideration must be given to the option of seeking place-of-safety orders. Social workers should not under any circumstances rely on a mother, already laden with awesome burdens, to get rid of a perpetrator whom they themselves are reluctant to face.

As of yet the law does not subscribe to the desirability of having too many options in the approach to perpetrators. In the meantime, however, social workers can still achieve much merely by reflecting upon their experiences of perpetrators in the past; it is most likely they will know that lightning, ill-informed, inadequate responses to perpetrators have compounded their task of rescuing and ensuring adequate care for their victims.

8
Starting afresh: the case of Sarah and Elizabeth

Introduction

The implication of previous chapters is that comprehensive and effective policies and strategies for *all* child sexual abuse cases do not and cannot exist; there are far too many types of cases and often far too many complex, challenging and unrelated components in each case. There has been much pretence to the contrary, in literature, research and training, but on examination this pretence has been easily exposed.

All the other chapters in this book implicitly and explicitly argue for the need to identify, discriminate, categorize and prioritize. The objective is for social workers and their managers in particular to face up honestly to the daunting task of recognizing the sexually abused child whose social and family context, in which the abuse takes place, is such as to make it potentially the most damaging abuse; pose the greatest challenge to the agencies involved; and create the most difficult obstacles in the way of rescuing the child and ensuring an alternative and adequate standard of care for his or her physical, emotional psychological and social development.

This chapter is going to identify such a case. It is then going to seek a philosophical base inclusive of ethical considerations. Policies will be constructed on this base, and strategies planned. The first task is to examine the principal characteristics of each of the components in this case, i.e. the child's vulnerability, the mother of the child, the perpetrator and the environment in which the abuse took place. The second, to re-establish and re-emphasize a particular framework of response, consisting of: the referral phase; the investigation phase; the intervention phase; the case conference phase. 'Disclosure' has dominated child sexual-abuse work, to the detriment of this framework of response. The reasons for this need to be explored, to allow social workers and their managers to commit themselves to the crucially important tasks of competent referral taking, systematic and well-prepared investigation, strategy-based intervention and meaningful case-conference preparation.

The chapter will return again to the case of Sarah and Elizabeth. The case will be dealt with strictly within these four phases of initial child sexual-abuse work. There will be intermittent discussion of challenging issues arising, e.g. interviewing small children without their parents' knowledge, developmental considerations in small children's responses to questioning, the use of anatomical dolls and the moments of greatest danger. The crucial role of the police will also be explored. Throughout the referral, investigation and intervention phases, reference will frequently be made to the criteria of *protection, family and social context* and *resources*. These criteria are central to social-work preparation for the case conference. The reasons for social workers' cynicism and lack of preparation for case conferences will be discussed. At the end of the chapter, social workers and their managers should be well prepared, not just for case conferences, but in knowledge, understanding and strategy, enabling them to provide a truly professional and effective response to the plight of children like Sarah and Elizabeth.

Who is the most vulnerable and damaged child?

In the absence of reliable empirical evidence, no one can say with certainty which sexually abused child has been the most vulnerable to abuse, nor what social and family context has compounded the damage it does and posed the greatest challenges to the agencies which have had to intervene. It is principally for that reason that I am going to rely on the experiences of some forty to fifty social workers working in an inner-city divisional office. It is situated in a densely populated area of South West Leeds. I work in that office, as a principal case worker for child abuse. A child sexual-abuse team is established there, as a consequence of the widely publicized child-sex rings which came to light in 1985/6 and the subsequent phenomenal increase in child sexual-abuse referrals. I have seen every such referral over a two-year period. I have supervised responses to a number of them and jointly responded with other colleagues. I have had lengthy discussions with every social worker and team leader in the office, exploring their views and feelings on the subject of this chapter. I have attended every child sexual-abuse case conference (and chaired many of them). I carry a limited caseload of child-abuse and child sexual-abuse cases. I also work as a consultant, trainer and initiator in various aspects of child abuse generally, in Leeds and elsewhere. Out of that experience and location, it is the unanimous view of my colleagues and myself that children in the approximate age range of two to seven, abused by their father or stepfather, constitute the most vulnerable, and potentially most damaged, sexually abused children, and, that the disclosure of such abuse is fraught with great risk and challenge for child, family and agencies alike.

Characteristics of the identified case

Vulnerability

A child between the age of two and seven is extremely vulnerable to sexual abuse, physically and psychologically. The child's intellect, cognition and perception are in what Piaget (Phillips 1981) would have referred to as the 'preoperational' levels of development in which the child has not yet acquired the 'mental structures needed for logical or abstract thought' (De Young 1986). Physically however, the two-year-old is fast reaching a level of self-control and motor co-ordination which enable him or her to respond and to act in the way that the perpetrator wants; the younger the child below two years of age, the more limiting is that ability. Sexual intercourse is a rare abuse perpetrated against children generally (Finkelhor 1984; Baker and Duncan 1985); it is an extremely rare abuse perpetrated against this age range in particular. Oral and manual masturbation, however, is very commonly perpetrated against very young children. From two onwards, the child is increasingly capable of performing this task on the abuser. Another more basic reason for the child's physical vulnerability is the fact that he or she cannot resist any physical coercion on the part of the perpetrator.

The psychological vulnerability is manifest in the extreme power imbalance between perpetrator and any child within this age range. The child is totally dependent upon the perpetrator in any abusing situation, knows and feels that dependency, and cannot, even if he wanted, run away from it. The child's perception of the perpetrator is one of mighty, all-embracing power. The perpetrator's size, strength and mobility, the sound of his voice, the money in his pocket, the goodies at his finger tips – all of these intensify a perception of power that the child feels obliged to respect.

Intellectually and cognitively, the child is incapable of realizing the meaning and extent of abuse; more importantly, he or she cannot predict or anticipate it nor have any conception of desire on the part of the perpetrator, nor of the strategies which the latter may devise for fulfilling those desires. The child's preoperational levels of development render him or her at the mercy of adult perpetrators who have literally hundreds of ways and means of exploiting that limited development. For example, the perpetrator can easily create a situation in which the three-year-old's compulsive curiosity is provoked without the child experiencing any sense of wrongdoing or danger. The perpetrator can also ensure that pleasure and rewards are intertwined with each stage of the manipulative process. Many perpetrators are unaware of the fact that their eventual ensnaring of their child victim is based upon sound, well-tested, behaviourist principles.

Mothers

For social workers the mothers of abused children in this age group are more likely to be carrying the additional burdens of family poverty, other children and totally unsatisfactory relationships with the abuser. Because of the poverty, and, sometimes because of the unsatisfactory relationships, much importance can be given to mother's part-time or full-time employment. This is nearly always of a domestic, factory or retail type. It is highly significant as a factor in the degree of protection that a mother has been able to provide for her child.

There is no evidence whatsoever to suggest that a mother's participation or collusion in the sexual abuse of her two-to-seven-year-old child(ren) is anything other than the most extreme rarity. The examples of mothers' sexually abusing their own children, which have been mentioned in previous chapters, can be safely interpreted as aberrations, having little or no significance for the training of professionals in working with child sexual abuse. The unwitting facilitation of the abuse is another matter, and many mothers are both shocked and full of guilt and remorse as a consequence of the realization that their absence and/or their trust of the perpetrator were major contributory factors. As we have seen in the first chapter, the 'apparent collusion' of a mother in the abuse of her child may be wrongly interpreted as such and is more likely to be an understandable reaction to insensitive, bungling intervention.

The father/stepfather perpetrator

The father/stepfather perpetrator of abuse against this young child may appear to function quite normally, as a breadwinner, a parent, a husband, a neighbour, etc. Beneath that veneer he is more likely to be a pathetic, weak, socially isolated individual who has never had any real bonding with the child, is likely to have little or no satisfactory sexual relationship with his wife, is incapable of having the same with any other adult, is generally powerless and inadequate in ordinary social contexts and who has stumbled upon the sense of power and achievement to be gained through the sexual abuse of those children totally dependent upon him. The cunning and stealth by which the abuse is perpetrated is no accurate measure of his intelligence; rather it is merely a further indication of the lack of sophistication and of the vulnerability of his victim.

The environment

The vast majority of such abused children who are referred to social workers will live in economically deprived areas. Social workers and many other child-care professionals frequent these areas. There is widespread poverty, environmental dilapidation, delinquency, family fragmentation and recon- stituted families on a massive scale. The high profile of social workers and police in areas like these can have a profound effect upon the course of events when allegations of child sexual abuse are made. (The problems and obstacles arising are likely to be magnified by the exposures made in the

Cleveland report, and by the subsequent emergence of parental pressure groups demanding official reports into their own particular cases.) In this environment the community and non-abusing family members alike are borne down with so many preoccupations that good, consistent and highly protective child care is the exception rather than the rule. Mother bears the brunt of all the ensuing consequences, for example, keeping child-protection agencies at bay (many of the allegations of child sexual abuse will be made about children and families already on the caseloads of social workers; as we have already seen (in the previous chapter) husbands are seldom about when professionals call, an absence which is more of a relief than regret to the latter); being far more bonded to their children than their partners are and, therefore being more conscious of their children's privations; being encouraged or compelled to seek part-time employment, and reluctantly relying upon her husband or friend or relative to care for the child.

The most significant characteristic about environments like these and the families which live in them, however, is another kind of power imbalance. It is similar in one respect to the power imbalance between perpetrator and victim: many individuals in these environments, including mothers, children and alleged perpetrators, perceive investigative and child-care agencies as mightily powerful, educated and articulate, influential, manipulative and threatening. Such perceptions are no mere paranoia; that power imbalance is a fact. In the light of the Cleveland report social workers in particular can be assured that these perceptions will be more acutely felt and will complicate their tasks substantially. Just as the power imbalance between perpetrator and victim is a source of much of the legal and moral condemnation of the act of abuse, so too should professionals be acutely aware of their ability to take advantage of the power imbalance between the established governmental bureaucratic edifices which employ them and the largely deprived, fragmented, uneducated and inarticulate families and communities in which they work.

Here then are the principal characteristics of the child victim, parents and social environment which are commonly found when allegations or sus-picions of the sexual abuse of this particular age group are made. Social workers should be able to respond on the basis of a humane and coherent philosophy, sound policy and effective strategy.

The philosophy underpinning child sexual-abuse work

Philosophy is a coherent system of values, ethical principles and convictions upon which policy is based. The literature of child sexual abuse is conspicuously lacking in any mention of philosophy. The Cleveland report demonstrates that that tragedy owed much to the non-existence of an established, recognizable, and respected philosophical base. No doubt, in Cleveland and elsewhere, social workers might respond to the question

'Define the philosophy underpinning your work', by replying: 'The protection of the child is paramount' or 'The department must always act in the best interests of the child'. Without context and an ethical framework, these are mere catchphrases, no more constituting a philosophical base than providing criteria and guidance for staff confronting enormously complex problems.

We have identified a complex and challenging case: the sexual abuse of children between the ages two to seven by a father or stepfather. We must be certain therefore about the philosophical basis of our actions. Chapter 3 discussed three distinct perspectives on child sexual abuse, the feminist, family-systems theory, and the humanist; each of them embraces values and convictions. The humanist perspective is the one that comes nearest to providing social workers in British social-services departments with the soundest, most relevant philosophical base. It evolves from a profundity and humility which acknowledges the potential for good and evil in each of us. It rightly implies (and Giarretto explicitly states it about himself) that we are all capable of sexually abusing children (far short of claiming that all men are capable of abusing their own children). It does not seek cause, blame or responsibility in abstractions like male-dominated societal structures or in dysfunctional family relationships revolving around a colluding mother. It lays great emphasis upon the necessity for rigorous, painful and honest self-scrutiny about our feelings for perpetrators.

In addition to that profundity and humility then, the broad values and convictions of a philosophical base should include the following:

1 There is no merit whatsoever in exposing child sexual abuse, if there is neither the will, the commitment nor the resources to combat it effectively.
2 Children should be protected from any form of abuse by any individual, family, community or agency. (But there are varying degrees of 'the need to be protected'. A fifteen-year-old girl having intercourse with the neighbour's son is much less in need of protection than the five-year-old boy being violently and persistently buggered by his father.)
3 This 'protection' principle must not be applied merely to rescue a child from one abusing situation, if her only destiny is to be abused in a different way in another.
4 Child sexual abuse is not the most traumatic or damaging form of abuse which children suffer. Most of the abuse (digital penetration, oral and manual masturbation, fondling, etc.) is infinitely less serious than many other categories of abuse which actually threaten the lives of children. This conviction is stressed, not to underplay the traumas endured by sexually abused children, but to re-emphasize the importance of realizing that such abuse seldom warrants the drastic and damaging action of removing children.
5 Young children are unable to articulate the value and benefit they derive from the myriad of facets of family and community life. The abuses which

such families inflict upon them are far more easily articulated. Patience, time and effort should not be spared in seeking the most accurate assessment of the child's family and social context. (The Cleveland report states: 'It is a sad fact that in very few of the social work files of the families seen by us, was there evidence of social workers taking a full social history of the family so as to inform both their own views and more widely, those of the case conferences they attended' (Butler-Sloss 1988: 75).)

6 Child sexual-abuse policy and strategy must be family oriented. Narrow dogma which seeks to focus entirely upon a particular individual in the abusing situation, e.g. the child or the perpetrator, is certain to exacerbate the crisis generated by the disclosure of child sexual abuse.

Philosophy and the law

Philosophy must evolve within the existing framework of law. But as we have already seen in Chapter 3, philosophy and law may not be compatible. Even more so is this the case in Britain where there has been virtually no departure by police and judiciary from the strictly punitive approach to perpetrators. The consequences of this limited response are, however, being recognized, as is evident in the Cleveland report, and in numerous articles and broadcasts made around the time of its publication. In Cleveland, as in most locations, the police held tenaciously to their right and to their duty of investigating a most serious crime, and of prosecuting the offender. They had neither intention nor inclination to share that task with other professionals (Butler-Sloss 1988: 49). Nor have police in general much appreciation of the occasional disastrous consequences of the 'success' of their actions, i.e. the removal and imprisonment of perpetrators, upon the child victims they seek to help. The philosophical base of child sexual-abuse social work has to revolve around this awareness and appreciation. This incompatibility is not unique in police–social-work relationships. On the contrary, as Thomas (1986) makes clear, the convictions of social workers determining their responses to many client groups, e.g. juvenile delinquents, the mentally ill and the elderly confused, are more often than not in stark contrast to the convictions of police officers advocating entirely different courses of action. Each profession can argue that they are merely upholding the law. And so they are, according to their own interpretations of the law. Social workers' weakness in the child sexual-abuse field has been not to argue that very same point: i.e. that they are upholding many child-protection and child-care laws by objecting to lightning strikes, the immediate removal of the alleged perpetrator, even worse, the removal of the victim, and the successful prosecution which may sentence that victim and his family to a debilitating guilt, shame and penury.

Once a philosophical base has been established, policy and procedures can now be declared and strategies planned. These may best be done, however, through experience of dealing with an actual case from the category that has been identified as potentially the most serious and most challenging. We will use the case of Sarah and Elizabeth from the first chapter. It is hoped that much has been learnt in subsequent chapters to enable us to formulate the most comprehensive policies and to devise the most effective strategies.

Re-establishing the framework for action

The exposure of child sexual abuse in recent years has led to a damaging and fundamental change in the structure of child-abuse work. Twenty years of practice had established a certain framework, comprising the **referral** phase, the **investigation** phase, the **intervention** phase and the **case-conference** phase. For social-services departments this framework has proved highly effective in the management of cases; for social workers it has helped to identify and separate the complex issues in each phase and facilitated strategies for coping with them. More importantly, it is a framework that has given workers confidence, enabling them to avoid being overwhelmed by a crippling sense of 'unmanageability'.

Child sexual-abuse literature and training has greatly undermined this framework. Crucially important phases like 'referral' and 'investigation', each demanding rigorous enquiry and tact, have become blurred and subsumed in what has become the dominant, all-pervasive component in child sexual-abuse work, namely disclosure. Child sexual-abuse training invariably means 'how to get a disclosure' (Metropolitan Police and Bexley 1987; Wakefield 1988). Child sexual-abuse literature is awash on the same topic. Glaser and Frosh (1988), for example, devote no less than twenty pages to the disclosure interview; the once crucially regarded 'referral' and 'investigative' phases do not even warrant a place in their index. The most significant indicator of this regrettable trend, however, is in the Cleveland report itself, where the goal of disclosure by the child is clearly seen to have become something of an obsession, an end in itself not only demolishing any systematic framework for response, but an end justifying some terrible means (the worst of which was denying small children access to their mothers on the grounds that those mothers may have been implicated in the abuse in some way or that their mere presence might inhibit the child from providing that much sought-after disclosure). The report states:

> Staff felt under pressure to seek confirmation from children of the diagnosis, or if the diagnosis was accepted by the professionals, to help children disclose the experiences they had encountered. The boundaries between diagnostic/assessment work and longer term therapeutic objectives were often confused.
>
> (Butler-Sloss 1988: 73–4)

Social work has always been vulnerable to novelty, to untested, unproven, dubious gimmickry. Thus the unedifying sight in social-services offices up and down the country of generic social workers and inexperienced, inexpert 'specialists' gathering their anatomical dolls, their drawing paper and crayons, and trying to operate their brand new video equipment, and then imposing themselves upon some hapless abused child, to emerge sometime later with an expression akin to Archimedes' when he roared 'Eureka!' Were social workers given any training and practice in this kind of work, and were it to provide vital evidence in court, then it might not be the source of criticism which it undoubtedly was in the Cleveland report. But exceptionally few social workers have had such training, and its use in court both here and in America has become increasingly and justifiably discredited.

Another far more serious reason for the popularity of 'disclosure work' has already been alluded to in previous chapters: social workers simply do not like having to face or to work with sexually abusing parents. How much more convenient and unchallenging it is in the comfortable confines of a clinic, an office, a school, a police station, gently and sensitively probing the child's experiences, without the presence of the parents. In my contacts with many authorities, I've been both astonished and depressed by the extent to which social workers and their team leaders have been seemingly unaware that this widespread practice is not merely an exploitation of the child's inability to resist, but also an effective way of concealing (from themselves) their own reluctance to face the parents.

Child sexual-abuse work must henceforth relegate 'disclosure' to the comparatively not so important status which it really has. It is nothing more than one of the many stages of the investigative process. It is much less challenging and complex than most others. Child sexual-abuse work should not revolve around disclosure; it should be based upon a rigorous categorization process, similar to that provided in Chapter 6. The principal components in that categorization were: *protection, family and social context, resources*. The issues surrounding these components and the criteria for assessing them lay the foundation upon which to proceed through referral, investigation, intervention and case-conference phases. Throughout each of these phases, we must always be exploring the protection, family and social context, and resources issues. The social worker's report to the case conference which will follow must demonstrate that such issues have been thoroughly explored, and that the department's view's and contributions to the conference are based upon that exploration.

The referral phase

Definition and policy

A child sexual-abuse referral is one that officially records any allegation or suspicion of sexual abuse or any concern about the welfare of a child whose appearance and/or behaviour indicates the possibility of sexual abuse. Departmental policy must stress the absolute necessity of a thorough completion of its referral form when such allegations, suspicions and concerns are expressed. (There is unfortunately enormous discrepancy in the quality of these forms. I have seen one type that doesn't even have a space for details of the family! Another dangerously excludes letting any subsequent worker know whether or not the child and family are aware of the referral being made. It is hoped that these departments' managers have read the Cleveland report.)

Another preoccupation besides disclosure work has blurred and undermined the importance of referral-taking, namely, joint working with other agencies, particularly the police. Whatever the difficulties in Cleveland, joint working is being vigorously pursued throughout the country. This has created the impression that *all* child sexual-abuse work is and should be done jointly. This is a nonsense. Just as the police rightly believe that there are still many aspects of child sexual-abuse work that is entirely their responsibility, so too should social-work managers accept the same about their front-line staff. Good referral-taking has always been a major goal in social-work education and training. It should be restated and re-emphasized in departmental child sexual-abuse policy. Whether one is going to investigate jointly or not should not be allowed to diminish the importance of the referral upon which the investigation is based.

Procedures in responding to a child sexual-abuse referral

There are 'organizational' and 'professional' procedures in responding to child sexual-abuse referrals. The former includes:

1 asking the referrer every question necessary to complete the referral form.
2 checking if the child or family is known to the department; in particular, if the child is on the child abuse/protection register; or, if the alleged or suspected perpetrator is a known child-abuse offender. If so, in either case, seeking out the file and the worker previously involved.
3 informing the team leader/manager that the referral has been made.

The professional procedures are far more numerous and complex and necessitate an awareness of the virtually limitless types of child sexual abuse, the numerous possible sources of the referral, the age of the child, the number and ages of siblings, the nature of the alleged abuse, the identity of the (suspected) perpetrator and the location in which the abuse took place. Table 8.1 incorporates all these considerations, with an additional question as to the impact each has on the social worker.

Let us now explore these considerations and at the same time reassert professional procedures in referral taking, by applying them to the referral received some six chapters ago.

Every single category in table 8.1 has implications for the **investigation** which may follow, which, of course, is precisely why the social worker needs

Table 8.1 Exploring the various components of child sexual-abuse referral-taking and the impact upon the social worker

The child age/sex/siblings/handicap/special needs	Person making the referral	Perpetrator (alleged/suspected)	Nature and extent of alleged abuse	Observations/indicators causing concern and/or suspicion of sexual abuse	Location of alleged suspected abuse
0–1	relative	mother	soliciting	child says it happened	at home
2–7	neighbour	father	pornography	child acts out sexual activity	school
8–11	friend	stepmother	exhibitionism		surgery
12–16	GP	stepfather	inappropriate touching	child draws or speaks of sexual activity	clinic
....	teacher	grandparent	kissing		neighbourhood
male/female	HV	sibling	sexually embracing or fondling	child becomes withdrawn amongst peers	nursery
....	community nurse	aunt/uncle	masturbation	child seems depressed or unhappy	hospital
number of siblings	police	neighbour	cunnilingus		unknown
place in family?	psychiatrist	professional	fellatio	child reluctant to return home	other
....	child	putative father	intercourse		
special education	anonymous	cohabitee	buggery	child in pain after visiting toilet	
physical handicap	other	babysitter	father–daughter incest		
mental handicap		other	father–son buggery	semen on clothes of child	
		unknown	mother–son incest		

to record them. For example, the identity of the referrer has major implications for how both the alleged abusing parent and the non-abusing parent may respond to the investigating officer(s). Whether or not either of them knows the referral is being made is also important. The type of abuse which is being alleged or suspected may have a major impact upon the social worker, as will most certainly the relationship between the child and the abused perpetrator. In the case of Elizabeth, the categories would be: a child between the age of two and seven; female; referred by school teacher; a suspected father as perpetrator; type of abuse unknown; various behavioural indicators causing suspicion of sexual abuse; and the presumed location, the child's home.

How then, at this referral stage, might one want to categorize this case, in the light of the three major categorization components: *protection*, *child and family context*, and *resources*. Obviously the referral cannot yet be completed, but it does already have some indication of becoming a high-priority case:

- a very young child possibly being sexually abused by her father.
- nature of the sexual abuse unknown.
- non-abusing parent's attitude unknown.
- department lacking experienced, confident and knowledgeable staff.
- department does not have comprehensive, coherent, ethically sound, child sexual-abuse philosophy, policies and procedures.
- department lacking adequate fostering resources if needed.

It is precisely the *potential seriousness* of this case, combined with the department's shortcomings, which is likely to compel worker and manager to act more swiftly than they need to. In that particular case it meant dashing round to the school, ill prepared, anxious and having no sense of control over the crisis the worker was about to precipitate. There are various lines of enquiry to pursue here before any dash round to the school or any approach is made to see the child.

The seven lines of enquiry to be made in referral-taking

In receiving a child sexual-abuse **referral**, the social worker should enquire about:

- The abuse, or observations/indicators suggestive of abuse.
- Who the perpetrator is and what is known about him/her.
- What is known of the circumstances surrounding the abuse.
- What is known about the general standard of care provided by the parents, and about the parents/carers themselves.
- Is the child and/or parent aware that a referral is being made to social services? If not, why not? (The answer is usually the dreaded one: a parent is the suspected perpetrator. But the question should be asked nonetheless.)

- The general health of the child: what observations, knowledge, etc., can be elicited about the child's emotional social, physical, psychological and social life.
- What if any, is the nature and extent of other agency involvement?

In the case of Sarah, the indicators and observations, i.e. a sudden unexplained withdrawnness; reluctance to go home; clinging to the teacher; intimate drawings; discomfort after toilet, were very strongly suggestive of some kind of sexual abuse. Yet it is very important that the worker retains an open mind on the matter and (tactfully) scrutinizes these observations and indicators with the referrer. Have they all come at once? or over how long a period? Are they intermittent, or to be observed all day long, every day? Is the referrer aware of any event in the child's or the child's school or family life which could have some bearing on these observations?

At this referral stage no one is openly suggesting that father is a perpetrator, and no one is yet able to say that sexual abuse has actually taken place. Enquiries therefore on this matter can be postponed (unlike many referrals in which an individual is named as the perpetrator). Likewise the circumstances, i.e. the time and location in which suspected abuse may have taken place, the absence or presence of others besides the perpetrator, etc., can only be guessed at and may be taken up again during the **investigative** phase.

The standard of general care provided by the parents, however, is an enquiry which should be explored as rigorously as possible from the outset. The younger the child, the more important this enquiry is for determining the investigative strategy. School teachers are exceptionally well placed to answer many of the questions within that enquiry:

- What do school staff know generally about the child's home and family life?
- What impressions have they gained about the parental contribution to the child's educational development?
- Have the parents taken a genuine interest in their children's progress at school?
- Has the teacher ever suspected that Sarah has attended school burdened with parental problems at home?
- (Most important, since it is the school which is making the referral.) How would school staff describe their relationships with the parents and, if they know parent or parents particularly well, how do they think they will react to a possible **investigation**?

Similarly, school staff are well placed to comment on the numerous other aspects of Sarah's development. Observations and opinions on these should be sought about the past and the present. If school staff believe there is a marked difference between past and present, they should be encouraged to specify. Questions may include:

● How does Sarah normally function emotionally and socially in the classroom? Does she express the whole range of emotions in appropriate circumstances? Is she well integrated in the class generally, and in smaller peer groups in particular? Is she basically a happy child curious, uninhibited, friendly, humorous, or is she inclined to be alone, uninterested, shy, withdrawn and anxious?

● Does Sarah appear frightened or burdened about anything at home? Is there marital conflict or separation looming which may be causing severe psychological stress?

● How does Sarah normally perform in school work? Is she an achiever? an achiever without anxiety? an achiever under pressure? Is there any particular impediment to learning?

The final enquiry about other possible agency involvement is important too and may easily be forgotten or thought irrelevant to the existing (potentially very serious) child sexual-abuse **referral**. The social worker should enquire of the school and from the agency's own records as to any previous or present involvement by any other agency, and reasons for it.

The benefits of enquiry

It will take much tact and patience on the part of the social worker to convince the referrer at the end of a telephone that this kind of thorough referral taking is not meant to be an interrogation. Referrers will have to get used to it: a child sexual-abuse referral is far too dangerous to be left exactly as the referrer may want to leave it. In any case, the previous enquiries are no more nor less than professional practice demands; they should be the very least that other professionals – particularly school staff – should expect. Such enquiries are in everyone's interests; the referrer, the child, her family, the social worker, and the department. Their principal value, however, is in their influences upon the **investigative** processes. The social worker who rigorously and systematically enquires at the **referral** phase will find it that much easier to be rigorous and systematic during the more challenging investigative phase. To the referrer, the social worker's enquiries will convey a sense of knowledge, confidence and control, that can only be reassuring; referrers may well be very much involved and needed in the investigative phase, and their anxieties (the natural anxieties of all referrers of possible child sexual abuse) may be considerably assuaged if they are communicating with a social worker who, they believe, is quite clearly preparing the groundwork for possible action on behalf of the child. At some stage, a decision to interview the parents is likely to be made. A social worker who approaches either or both parents, knowing nothing more about them other than the fact that they are the parents of an allegedly sexually abused child, will be in a much less advantageous position to investigate properly than a worker who has made a thorough enquiry. The nature of that information gained by the latter worker should greatly influence the process and outcome of the interview with the parents. It should be instrumental in determining a strategy with the aim of securing the maximum co-operation of the non-abusing parent.

Information gained from enquiries

The referral enquiries elicit the following information and opinions from school staff.

- The father has recently lost his job. The mother has always had part-time employment. She works in a local supermarket.
- The staff have never had any previous cause to believe that there were problems at home between parents. Until recently, they believed that Sarah's usual happy state, her integration in the classroom, her average attainments, were indicative of a reasonable family home life. Her parents have attended parent evenings on a few occasions, have responded as requested to the numerous memos and letters circulated by the school. They are not well off by any means and have said 'no' repeatedly to the invitation for them to go on costly school trips. There is some indication of intensive involvement by Sarah's father in her liking for drawing; she has mentioned his praises many times, and it is obvious that her father is a keen amateur painter himself. Sarah has told staff that it was her father who taught her to draw pictures of naked bodies in intimate poses.
- Until recently, staff have never had cause to express concern about any obstacles to her social, emotional, psychological, physical or educational development. These recent behavioural changes and apparent distress, however, may be adversely affecting her educational development at least. Staff confirm that they observe only intermittent change, i.e. that Sarah's withdrawnness, her clinging and her discomfort on returning from the toilet, are not pervasive, i.e. not to be observed every day. They were observed on the day they made the referral (Friday), but the last occasion was during the previous week.
- Staff confirm that Elizabeth, Sarah's sister, has given them no cause for concern at any time.
- According to records, there hasn't been any previous involvement by social services or any other agency.

The investigation phase

The real and the ideal

The phenomenal increase in child sexual-abuse referrals has necessitated major reviews, restructuring, new policies and procedures for **investigation**. The most conspicuous initiatives to emerge have been the establishment of child sexual-abuse teams in a small number of authorities and joint investigation between police and social services. Where the latter initiative has stemmed from a combined analysis by police and social services of inadequate responses, and the subsequent evolution of comprehensive joint-working policies and procedures, then such an initiative has led to an immense improvement in investigative outcomes. But, as the Cleveland report clearly implies, most agencies have not yet undergone this critical analysis, have not yet 'formulated the basic principles and frameworks of its own practice', let alone developed sophisticated joint-working policies and procedures with other agencies. The following pages on **investigation** and **intervention** do not therefore attempt to describe or promote any ideal on joint working; rather, the aim is to explore and promote 'basic principles' and sound working practices for social workers working in social-services departments. That practice comprises attitudes, approaches, skills, techniques and objectives that are wholly compatible with the ethical principles of the profession, and with the statutory responsibilities of the authorities for whom they work.

Immediate responses

No one could dispute that this referral necessitates an **investigation**. But the timing and the method requires some careful planning. In the original example (Chapter 1), the social worker saw fit to visit the school immediately, with very little information. Consultation with three other professionals then took place and was followed by disclosure work with the use of anatomical dolls. These were three major blunders, ensuring that the mother of the child was going to be shocked and angry when she learnt about it. That would guarantee her resentment, distrust and total lack of co-operation. *A child in school should not be seen by a professional from outside the school without a parent's knowledge and permission.* This is a fundamental parental right. All kinds of reasoning and excuses can be concocted in defence of ignoring it; for example, the parents might be implicated; they might pressurize the child to protect them; they might prime the child for future interviews; the child might be sentenced to a lifetime's abuse, etc. And so might all these things happen. The glaring fact remains, however, that in this flagrant abuse of parental rights, supposedly in the interests of protection, the professionals are more likely to be exposing the child to the far greater danger of rejection by the non-abusing parent. Witness the trauma inflicted upon Sarah by a mother who, as a consequence of being denied that fundamental right, was unable to offer the warmth, love and reassurance that the child needed more than anything else (Chapter 1, p. 3).

The strategies of **investigation** for this particular category of case should be based upon a conviction that mothers do not normally sexually abuse their six-year-olds; that they do not consciously facilitate that abuse in any way; that they would be horrified to find out that their child was being sexually abused; that they would be particularly disgusted and angry on learning that the perpetrator was their husband or cohabitee; and that, if sexual abuse were confirmed, they would take every precaution to protect their child. The fact that there is a minute fraction of mothers who do sexually abuse their six-year-olds, or who consciously facilitate such abuse by their husbands, or who, on learning that their husbands are perpetrators, choose not to protect their child, should not deter social workers from reasserting and upholding the basic and fundamental parental rights of mothers.

Timing

There is no need for the worker to be mounting a full-scale investigation of this referral on the day it is received. Even less so, is there a need for the social worker to be dashing round to the school with a bagful of anatomical dolls. The head teacher of the school should be asked to invite the parents to the school to discuss her concerns. Since there is no evidence of sexual abuse, that aspect need not and should not be mentioned in the invitation. The social worker can arrange to be at the school if and when the parents attend. But the social worker should ensure that she has not met the child before meeting the parents.

The headteacher is not likely to welcome this plan. She would much prefer social workers to say 'It's our responsibility now' (and who could fault her for that, when she, like everyone else, senses that this could turn out to be a real mess, with her and her staff in the middle of it). Alternatively then, the social worker can visit the home, inform parents of the receipt of the referral, discuss the teacher's concerns with them, and seek consent for an interview with the child in the presence of the mother.

This may appear to be an act of folly; it is in reality a respect for the parents which will almost certainly pressurize them into approving of an interview with the child, and, if recommended, a paediatric examination. How come?

Let's imagine that the father is the perpetrator. The first contact made by the school or the social worker is going to have alarm bells ringing in his ears. He is going to be feverishly thinking of a strategy of his own. The thought of a medical examination is going to terrify him. He will think he must resist that at all costs. But can he? And can he resist it too strongly without making his wife suspicious? How justified his refusal for a medical would appear, if social workers and teachers and other professionals had conducted an investigation behind his back, and a police officer had arrived at his door. But in this case he and his wife have been treated with the upmost respect – why, the social worker has refused even to see their child without their permission! And the social worker is in their home right now merely to share with them some of the observations and concerns of the school staff. These concerns are worrying because, as the school staff have made clear,

Elizabeth and Sarah come from a good home, from obviously responsible caring parents. That is why their children have never been a source of concern before. Indeed, the staff have complimented the parents, just as the social worker will do now, again and again throughout the interview.

It is unlikely that either parent is going to prevent a worker who treats them with this respect from interviewing the child, without giving the very powerful impression of gross unreasonableness and 'something to hide'; nor can the non-abusing parent, on hearing of the very substantial and worrying changes in her daughter's behaviour, feel justified or comfortable in refusing the recommendation of a paediatric examination. (My own particular strategy is never to suggest that the child has been sexually abused, but to describe and emphasize the dramatic changes in the child's behaviour in such a way that clearly implies that possibility. Then, to ask the parents how they might explain the behaviour and, if they can't, to ask them if they can think of anyone else who might be able to. In this particular case, with a child in pain and discomfort after micturition, a doctor is the only answer, but it is important to ensure that it is the mother's answer, not the social workers.)

It requires much confidence and flexibility to implement this strategy. The worker appears somewhat naïve but in reality is engaging in a difficult struggle of power and manipulation with the alleged perpetrator. Social workers are no different from other professionals in not wanting to appear naïve. They are, after all, supposed to be professionals. It is much easier for social workers to immerse themselves in an investigative process that revolves entirely around the child and totally excludes the parents. This 'secrecy' is quite ironical, considering that child sexual-abuse literature makes much play of the sustained secrecy of sexually abusing families. There is a mutual convenience in secrecy between the family abuser who does not want anyone to know about the abuse, and those professionals who are reluctant to let parents know they are questioning their child about that abuse.   The reputable Metropolitan Police and Bexley Experiment (1987) may recognize the dangers; it has established well-tested procedures for avoiding them; after the referral stage it states: 'Visit the family. . . . Seek consent for interview of the child, medical examination, use of video recording . . .' (p. 7).

Interviewing children aged two to seven

The 'success' of the social worker in chapter 1 in gaining a disclosure from the child should not be allowed to conceal the fact that it was exceptionally bad practice to interview her so soon, in that location, and when she was in a confused state provoked by the anxiety of well-intentioned adults all around her. Such a 'disclosure' is worthless as evidence for prosecution. Interviewing Sarah should only take place in an environment in which she feels safe, and at a time when she can demonstrate to an observer that she is without tension, fear and confusion. That initial interview raises a number of issues which need to be clarified before proceeding with the investigation. These are: developmental considerations, and the use of anatomical dolls.

Developmental considerations

The most important outcome of an interview is generally assumed to be when the child actually names a perpetrator and describes a particular act of abuse. This assumption is based upon a conviction that has no scientific validity, and yet which has occupied a pivotal position in child sexual-abuse literature and training, namely, that *the child must always be believed.* Regrettably, this is another conviction stemming from the literature's and trainers' failure to categorize child sexual abuse and to realize that different categories of children perceive and articulate experiences in different ways, that certain categories of children are more capable of imagining than others, fantasizing, exaggerating, lying, and/or being manipulated or forced to lie. The two-to-seven-year-old category is one that demands much caution and discrimination in interpreting whatever replies a child may give. (Three times in twelve months I have encountered allegations of specific acts of abuse by three- and four-year-olds which could not be supported by medical evidence; in two of those cases, after investigation, the paediatrician and social worker (rightly) did *not* believe the child. That is not to say that the children were not sexually abused, but merely that they were not abused in the way they described. This can be a crucial matter in investigation, prosecution and long-term management of the case). Fortunately for us in Britain, America has painfully learnt this lesson, and has already directed research towards establishing ways and means of assessing the truthfulness of statements made by very young children. De Young (1986) has produced a conceptual model for this purpose. It outlines a series of investigative steps to 'assess the type and quality of information about both the alleged abuse and the child's development that are needed at each step to increase or decrease the index of suspicion that the sexual abuse did occur' (p. 551). The model is specifically aimed towards the two-to-seven age group and is of such a quality and rarity in child sexual-abuse literature that it warrants something more than a fleeting reference.

De Young tests the clarity, celerity, certainty and consistency of the child's allegation. On clarity, she explores the development factors pertinent to children of this age: 'characterized by a cognitive style that would work significantly against clarity . . . their perception and definition of an object [is] in relation to its particular function'; their inability to understand that 'objects remain the same despite a change in physical appearance . . .', the 'tendencies for concreteness and egocentrism also will cloud an allegation . . .' and (p. 552):

> Pervasive transductive reasoning which causes a child to reason from
> one particular idea to another without logically connecting them,

creates a vague free associative style of communication, which, further encumbered by difficulties with language, precludes any real clarity.

It should be stressed that this is not meant to encourage professionals to doubt that sexual abuse has taken place; on the contrary, they should understand that the considerable developmental factors preclude the child from giving a clear and convincing account of it. On celerity, De Young concludes that the child cannot be expected to report at once if she is being sexually abused. There are numerous reasons not to expect this, the most obvious one being the pressure for secrecy placed on the child by the offending adult. 'Delays in disclosure therefore . . . should not be used as a rationale for doubting the truthfulness of an allegation.' De Young highlights the developmental factors which preclude a child from fantasizing about sexual abuse: 'fantasies of a child of this age are generally reflective of wishful thinking and are so bound to the pleasure principle that they invariably have a hedonistic tone . . . fantasies at this age stress mastery and competence: that is, the child as hero and as problem solver, as victor rather than victim' (p. 553). De Young concludes:

> These developmental aspects of fantasy and imagination then, argue against a young child fantasizing about being sexually abused . . . the more details a child can give, the more negative in feeling the experience is that is being related and the more the child describes sexual acts that exceed in maturity, sophistication and ability what would be considered normal for that child's psychosocial level of development (after the variables of class, culture, and individual differences are taken into account), the more likely is the child to be describing real as opposed to imaginary events.

The second step of this model elicits 'elaborated details' from the child about various aspects of the alleged abuse; due attention is first given to the amount and nature of sexual knowledge the child has before the alleged offence took place (which is a very good reason for sharing with a non-abusing parent before the interview takes place). The aspects include: specific actions during the abuse; the context in which it took place, i.e. identity of perpetrator, time, location; details about secrecy surrounding the abuse; and 'affective' details, i.e. the child's emotional responses to the act and to the perpetrator. On these last aspects, the interviewer should seek out the level of congruence between the feelings of the child about the abuse and the feelings/pressures she experiences because of the secrecy surrounding it:

> For instance, if a young child describes feeling hurt by an act of digital penetration, but feeling happy about the toy he or she got for keeping the secret, there is a high level of congruence between detail and feeling.
>
> (p. 555)

De Young believes the child 'is likely to judge a person by possessions or appearance rather than by behaviour'. Thus a child, after describing 'a painful act of molestation in a frightening context', may then 'portray as nice an alleged perpetrator who has a new car or video games for the television'.

The next step is to consider the 'behavioural indicators' of the child, as they have evolved in the literature in recent years. De Young cautions however: 'there is little consistency among the various indicator lists. The net effect is a kind of *mélange* – a veritable grab bag of indicators that potentially lends itself to much abuse and most certainly to false positive identifications' (p. 555). De Young recommends Finkelhor and Browne's (1985) conceptual model of indicators. The final steps in De Young's model consider the 'vulnerability of the child' and the possible 'motivation for lying'.

It will be obvious from this review of the model that the author's principal concern is not to spread a belief that small children cannot be relied upon. De Young's work obviously springs from an acute consciousness of the sloppy, unplanned, unstructured way that the young abused child has often been approached and questioned by professionals from different agencies, particularly the police and child-protection agencies, and the subsequent humiliations in court and elsewhere to which many small children have been subjected as a consequence (Rush 1980). De Young's model, rather than instilling doubt in the professional's mind, provides a comprehensive, systematic and detailed method of adding considerable weight and substance to the professional's intuitive conviction that a child actually has been abused. It is one of the very rare such models and the only one constructed specifically for the age category under discussion.

The use of anatomical dolls

Anatomical dolls can facilitate valuable disclosure in interviewing very young children. Their effective use, however, depends to a large extent upon experience, skill and the personality of the worker using them. I have had the pleasure of working alongside a colleague who was highly effective in using these dolls. In watching her at work, and in discussing it with her, it is obvious to me that there are serious limitations to the effectiveness of a policy (or no policy) which allows workers to 'try their hand' with these dolls on their very young clients. This particular colleague had a remarkable empathy with small children in any situation, whether abused or not. She would spend any amount of time necessary to establish a relationship with the child, to create a relaxing atmosphere, a secure environment, a mutual trust and respect – all of this before even allowing the child to see the dolls (the impact upon the attempt to get a disclosure of the child's first sight of the genitals on these dolls is a matter which has as yet not been addressed; it is generally assumed, without evidence, that it can have no adverse impact). I have, on the other hand, seen untrained social workers and social workers and police officers combined, with no great attributes of empathy, attempting to gain their experience and skill using the dolls, in actual unsupervised disclosure work with children; I have seen children so tensed, and social workers so frustrated and agitated in their failure to get a disclosure, that the only outcome has been a guarantee that a worthwhile disclosure would never be made. For example, the immediate transportation of the allegedly abused child from its home and family, to 'play with the dolls' in the alien surroundings of a video-recording room, no matter how homely it is made to look, or how many nice friendly people may be there, is not exactly conducive to relaxing a four-year-old. Social Services must have a policy which prohibits the use of dolls by workers untrained in their use. If skilled and experienced workers are not available, then the department should not lend itself to participation in this phase of the investigative work. Similarly, with other 'disclosure' aids: drawings, miniature homes, puppets, etc., social workers and police officers should have undergone a basic minimum training in the use of such equipment, before attempting to use it in actual cases.

Mother's presence and support in disclosure work

Sarah's parents consent to the child being interviewed in her own home, by the social worker, in the presence of her mother. The father cannot resist this 'reasonableness' and is infinitely less secure and more accommodating than when he and his wife were confronted by a *fait accompli*, which united them in violent opposition to any further action by social services. The social worker praises them both for their own 'reasonableness', saying how easy it is to understand why these children have never been a source of concern to the teachers before. Obviously the mother will be pressing the social worker to say exactly what she thinks has happened to her daughter, to which the social worker can justifiably reply that that is precisely what she intends to find out, with her (the mother's help). Father may request or demand that he is present during the interview too, but the social worker can 'reason' with him as to how distracting this might be for the child, and, in any case, 'mothers' are always far more reassuring to small children being interviewed by strangers than are fathers. (In my experience, if father is a perpetrator, it is most unusual for him to 'demand' that he is present. The prospect of exposure is anxiety provoking enough without the prospect of exposure in his wife's and social worker's presence. But it need be no great problem if father does insist on being present; or indeed, even if he subtly or blatantly intimidates the child. An observant professional will note how he does so, and why; it will reassure the professional and help persuade the mother that he is indeed the perpetrator. Mother is then likely to support the intensive surveillance operation then necessary, between herself, the social worker, police and school.)

It is crucially important that mother is prepared for this interview. The social worker will give her a very good idea of what's likely to happen during it: first, mother will introduce the social worker to the child; then the initial 'getting to know the child'; creating the right atmosphere; the possible use of the dolls and drawings, etc., and, exploring with mother the level of awareness in Sarah about sexual matters, and self-protection against abuse, and what mother knows about the child's anatomical vocabulary. The younger the child within this particular age range, the more the worker may depend upon the use of the dolls; in this particular case, where a child of six and a half and the alleged abuser apparently share an interest in drawing human figures, and where this may have been exploited as a preliminary to sexual abuse, then discussion and play around drawings are likely to be an important component in the interview. Video recording might be suggested, in a way that mother realizes is reassuring to her and advantageous for the child. The decision then is mother's. Sarah will be acutely conscious of her mother's eyes, her ears, her thoughts, her facial expressions throughout this interview. All of these must convey the love and the reassurance that the mother can give. She must be advised against the very natural, yet unconscious expression of anger or disgust as she listens to her child; and, if need be, she can offer the child as much non-verbal encouragement as the social worker may indicate.

(Some may think that this is displaying a rather naïve faith in mothers, and that many mothers encountered by social workers simply would not be able to restrain a natural anger and explosiveness as a consequence of the visit by the social worker, and that this anger must at some time manifest itself, if not against Sarah directly, then at least in her presence. This thinking, however, is more of a lack of faith in one's ability to relate to and to win over the support of mother during this crisis-laden investigative time. Thus the easier, more convenient distrust of and exclusion of mother.)

The crisis of disclosure

Sarah discloses in much greater detail the abuse to which she has been subjected over a very long time. There is no suggestion of intercourse; there has been fondling, mutual and manual masturbation, oral sex, and frequent and sustained watching of hard-core pornographic videos. Sarah is not aware of anything similar ever happening to her sister Elizabeth. The 'secret' was to be kept from both Elizabeth and her mother. (This may, of course, be a clever tactic on the part of the perpetrator, who may be abusing Elizabeth as well. But there is not the slightest indication that he is, either from the teachers who have been closely observing her over many days, or from anyone else. There can be no justification therefore for subjecting Elizabeth or her mother to an additional investigation). It is exceedingly difficult for the social worker to continue with this disclosure work, at the same time as having to monitor its effect upon mother's self-control and maintenance of her support and encouragement of her child. She is obviously shocked and angry by the disclosure – even the sight of the drawings her daughter has done at her father's request shock her. However difficult the disclosure has been for the child (made much less difficult by this preparation and by ensuring mother's support), it is the child's mother who is in greater need at this moment in time. And yet (as was all too painfully obvious in that first chapter), the child needs her mother's visible strength and support *particularly* at this moment. Having anticipated all these factors the worker will have prepared a number of contingencies for dealing with them (for example, if the disclosure was so devastating for mother that she may need a brief separation and solitude from the interview, then a separate room, helpful colleague, tea/coffee, etc., should be available for this purpose, the intention being to allow her to recover as quickly as possible so that she can return to the child).

Mother consents to the child having a medical examination. The social worker asks her to reassure Sarah that this medical isn't some kind of punishment because of the disclosure she has given. The mother is prepared for the paediatric examination just as carefully as she was prepared for the disclosure interview. She is told about the paediatrician's standard practice of photographing the child in very explicit postures. She is asked to consider that now, and to decide whether or not she approves of it. Like nearly all mothers she will not have the confidence to protest or resist in the clinic unless she has prepared herself to do so. If she considers it, doesn't want it and yet feels that she will be unable to say so, then the social worker can offer to speak on her behalf. The social worker will also inform mother that, if she disagrees with the doctor's opinion, she is perfectly entitled to request a second opinion. It is highly unlikely that she would do so when she has been so instrumental in the disclosure work. But the principle should be underlined in social-services policy in any case, namely, *that any member of the public has a right to seek a second medical opinion on any health matter.* As far as medical diagnosis of child sexual abuse is concerned, the depressing disagreements amongst doctors actually enhances the social-work assessment of the indicators and the impact of sexual abuse; where a medical diagnosis claims that a child has been seriously sexually abused, and there are no behavioural, emotional, educational indicators which would support that diagnosis, then the social worker is perfectly entitled to encourage parents to seek a second medical opinion.

The intervention phase

Categories of intervention

A social worker(s) may intervene in anyone or more of the following ways:

1 Arranging a medical and transporting child and mother to hospital.
2 Informing the police. Joint planning, visits and action.

3 Removal of the child through a place-of-safety order and placement in a foster home.
4 Removal of the child through a request from mother for voluntary care or advising/recommending this course of action to mother.
5 Counselling of mother and perpetrator, with a view to obtaining the voluntary removal of the latter.

Some may be surprised to see medical examinations classified as 'intervention'. The child and family will certainly perceive a paediatric examination as a massive intervention. In most cases the police will already be aware of social-services involvement (if the proper referral procedures have been adhered to), but it is now imperative for the police to be informed that a medical opinion is being sought on a child who has disclosed sexual abuse. The removal of the child through either voluntary care or place-of-safety order is the most drastic action. The voluntary removal of an alleged perpetrator will largely depend upon the nature and quality of the investigation; how the police conduct their own investigation; the degree of mutual co-operation between police and social services; and the interviewing skills and confidence of a social worker (and police officer if involved).

The moment of greatest danger

We can presume that in the case of Sarah, the paediatric examination supports the child's disclosure. The crisis for both the child and the mother is intensifying. It may also be intensifying dangerously so for the father who must await in terrible fear, shame and possibly self-hatred, to an extent that he may periodically feel compelled to inflict the ultimate punishment upon himself. This, regrettably, seldom enters the heads of professionals at this dangerous moment in time, and training courses are light years away from ever considering it. The social worker must plan a strategy based around *the actual anticipation that it will happen*, in order to ensure that the child will in no way be involved or be a witness to such self-destruction by a loved one. Again the mother's role is crucial; she is not a psychiatrist, but it would be well worth asking her for her opinion on how her husband might react to the overwhelming evidence of abuse. She may not know; she may be too traumatized herself even to think about it; but, on the other hand, she may have many memories of how he has reacted to other crises in their lives that might give some clues to how he is going to react to this one. Because of this uncertainty and danger, it is vitally important that the police interview with the perpetrator takes place before the child returns to the home. The social worker can be perfectly frank with mother on this matter; the latter will find it easy to understand; amidst the anger and disgust she is likely to be feeling, she may also be experiencing some suicidal impulses herself. But at this stage, because of the way the **referral**, **investigation** and **intervention** in this case have been carried out and because of her centrality in each phase, she will also realize the overwhelming need her child has for her at this dangerous moment.

The police investigation

It has been made clear earlier in this chapter that the goal is not to portray some ideal method of joint **investigation and intervention** which will always succeed. The primary objective was to use this particular (heavily disguised) case to explore what is right and appropriate in the thinking and actions of social workers, and in the philosophy and policies of the social-services departments for which they work. That has been done almost to the extent of completion but, now that the police are involved and will conduct their own investigation in their own way, we must acknowledge that the ultimate objective of police and social workers is mutual co-operation and joint working of the highest order, from the earliest stages. That would necessitate a *joint exploration* of each agency's philosophy and policy towards the whole field of child sexual abuse; the search for common ground, the evolution of joint working practices through investigation, intervention and case-conference phases. Some social services and police authorities have made much progress in this respect, notably Metropolitan Police and Bexley (1987), but the vast majority have not; have not even begun the necessary task (as was the case in Cleveland) of a rigorous analysis of their own policies and practices in child sexual-abuse work, let alone the far more difficult task of hammering out a philosophical base for under-pinning mutually agreed policies and strategies for joint working by both agencies. Casual and friendly working relationships between senior or middle management in each of these agencies is no substitute for the rigorous, disciplined, systematic and ruthlessly honest exercise which is needed.

Given that sorry state of affairs, all the actions and progress described throughout this chapter may come to nought, if the investigating police officers are not aware of the thinking behind it, or, if they are aware of it and have no sympathy with it. Worse than that, the police may so easily and unwittingly sabotage that progress, if they have been deliberately left out of the preceding action. Needless to say then, it is not the author's intention to advocate lone working in child sexual-abuse work; on the contrary, that in itself is an act of folly guaranteed *not* to be in the child's interests and very likely to exacerbate existing frictions and suspicions between the two agencies.

The police role is absolutely crucial to the welfare of the child and for the long-term management of the case. At this point of greatest vulnerability and danger in the case as a whole, police action towards the perpetrator is the single most powerful factor in determining the outcome. If they perceive the perpetrator merely as 'another perpetrator' who needs to be locked up and hastily proceed with that one and only objective, then the risk of disaster is drastically increased. By disaster is meant at best that the whole strategy, upon which **referral**, **investigation** and **intervention** was based, will be in ruins; at worst, this father will kill himself, his wife will periodically blame the child and herself and end up in a psychiatric hospital, and Elizabeth and Sarah will eventually be permanently removed, to be subjected to a life of chaos, confusion and guilt, for which all the therapy in the world will be of no avail. (I'm sure I am only one of many social workers and police officers who have painful memories of such outcomes.) On the other hand, if a local police force is fully aware of, shares and respects, has jointly engaged in the planning and in the implementation of strategies aimed at securing the non-abusing parent's support and also fully realizes the fragility and danger present at this moment, then that same police force will approach the perpetrator in an entirely different way. That, of course, must be the objective, and the process by which it is eventually achieved must begin from within the police force itself. The police should not be tempted, as social services and other agencies have been, into the charade of 'from now on we will work much closer with social workers in child sexual-abuse cases'. Just as this and previous chapters have sought to encourage rigorous self-analysis within each social-services department and area office, so too must the police do the same; perhaps even more so, because more is actually required from them: a significant widening of their role from the purely investigative, prosecutory one to that of child-welfare and protection in their most challenging sense.

The removal of this particular perpetrator, either voluntarily or other-wise, may present a major challenge to both agencies. But again, because of the way that the **investigation** and **intervention** have been carried out, there is a much greater prospect of removing him without generating the type of catastrophes – for both child and family – that have been all too familiar in recent year. Remove him to where? Here is a major *resources* issue which will have to be tackled in the interests of sustaining the strategy of enlisting mother's support and approval. Might that support not be sorely tested by a simple demand that her husband gets out, 'goes wherever hell he likes'? Not only do we risk losing mother's support with this attitude, but it is in fact a flagrant contradiction of many of the principles and policies upon which the **referral**, **investigative** and **intervention** strategies are based. Yes, he has committed vile, disgusting acts of abuse against his own daughter, and he has committed serious acts of crime. But this perpetrator is something more, and no one would better testify to that fact than Sarah herself. We will find out in due course precisely what else this man is besides an abuser, and what precisely is his overall contribution to Sarah and her family. In the meantime, however, social services and police combined should be explor-ing the provision of temporary accommodation for perpetrators specifically for this type of case. (This is a mandatory provision in Giarretto's and some other American programmes.) It can minimize the degree of shame felt by all family members; it can therefore reduce the risk of catastrophic action by the perpetrator in particular; and, perhaps most important of all, it can sustain mother's support for the way in which the case is being handled and therefore increase the pressure upon the perpetrator to make this move voluntarily. All of these possible advantages are wiped away and the risks of catastrophe heightened considerably if the police response to that much sought after admission by the perpetrator is to put him behind bars for an indefinite remand period, to be followed by trial, conviction and imprisonment.

No agency, of course, is more aware of this fact than the police themselves. And with no less a person than Lord Justice Butler-Sloss herself advocating that 'some fathers [perpetrators] should be allowed to remain at home' (Child Sexual Abuse International Conference, 23 September 1988), we can confidently predict that significant changes in law and in procedure will soon enable the police to act in the way that each and everyone of them seeks to do: in the interests of the protection and welfare of the child. Sarah is the child, and her father the perpetrator, whom Butler-Sloss undoubtedly had in mind when she made this statement.

The case-conference phase

The question of protection, family and social context, and resources

There is much doubt and cynicism about the function and usefulness of **case conferences** (Corby 1987). An obvious contributory factor is that they have increased at an alarming rate, mainly due to the exposure of child sexual abuse. This increased frequency has made it difficult for the professional participants to hold on to the fundamental principles and purposes of a case conference, even more, to sustain the effort, sincerity and commitment that it necessitates. Case conferences are seldom reviewed, analysed or tested. There is no in-built monitoring mechanism to warn participants that it has strayed far from principle or purpose. Strong leadership is helpful but, like the participants themselves, the leadership is seldom permanent, and the group dynamics are in a constant state of change. The end product of these deteriorating trends can only be a situation similar to that which occurred in Cleveland: as many as a dozen or more professional people collectively agreeing with the removal of children on the 'evidence' of a very brief medical examination, thereby making a mockery of the 'safeguarding through collective decision-making' principal function of case conferences. Child sexual-abuse literature and training have also contributed to the demise; case conferences are barely mentioned in whole textbooks, unwittingly pandering to an already widespread cynicism that these 'talking shops' have nothing to do with the real world of child sexual abuse. Little wonder, then, that social workers neither respect nor prepare well for case conferences.

Making case conferences serve a purpose

The importance of case conferences can best be appreciated by reflection upon the work of previous chapters, particularly chapter 6, on the categorization of child sexual abuse. A conceptual framework emerged from that chapter, constructed around the pillars of *protection*, *family and social context*, and *resources*. These are the crucial issues which have to be continuously assessed and reassessed throughout the referral, investigation and intervention phases. The professionals who attend the case conference must demonstrate that that assessment has taken place, and that the conclusions reached and the actions recommended are based upon it. For the reasons already given in Chapter 6, the social worker's contribution to that assessment is potentially the most valuable one. She has been totally involved in and has had major responsibilities during the referral, investigative, and intervention phases. The implication is clear: the value of the social worker's contribution to the conference and their confidence in making that contribution will depend largely upon their effectiveness during the three previous phases. If the protection, family-and-social-context and resources issues have been fully explored throughout those phases and if all actions have been based upon that exploration, it is highly likely that the social worker can produce a first-class report and sound recommendations for the conference. If, on the other hand, the social worker has been instructed merely to remove a sexually abused child, has placed the child with totally ill-prepared foster parents, left the natural parents devastated but united against social services and is expecting conference to advocate care proceedings, then it is unlikely that the worker can contribute anything of value to the conference.

As the case of Sarah has been conducted throughout this chapter, the social worker has the experience and knowledge to make a very valuable contribution to the case conference. Between the time of the probable removal of the perpetrator and the conference, the social worker will complete the assessment of the *family and social context* of the sexual abuse, using criteria similar to those in Chapter 6. The *protection* issue is very clear in this case. Table 6.1, (pp. 76–7) will illustrate that the case is a high-priority one in terms of protection. Elizabeth as well as Sarah needs to be protected, and every agency represented at the conference has an obligation to support mother in this role. Whilst father is away, that is a relatively easy task, but if the assessment of the family and social context concludes that his contribution towards Sarah in particular and the family in general is such that conference considers the possibility of his rehabilitation at some future date, then it should decide to reconvene nearer the time of his release to plan in detail how protection is going to be maintained. As for the *resources* issue, it has to be said that conference participants are not the most forthright or humble individuals in acknowledging the poor quality of provision to clients as a consequence of limited (or non-existent) resources. We have been given numerous examples of how limited resources can seriously impede professional practice. A short-sighted, unimaginative management, failing to produce a coherent and principled philosophy, workable sensible policies, a comprehensive categorization of child sexual abuse, and well-thought-out strategies for coping with the categories it regards as the most serious, is the worst of all limitations on resources. The worker in that department is not likely to have made a very good referral, carried out a thorough investigation nor intervened very effectively in the interests of the child. That same social worker can hardly feel confident in reporting to the case conference. A more conspicuous resource limitation is untrained, ill-prepared or non-existent foster parents. It is a pervasive feature of social-services life that is not likely to be admitted at a case conference. Unfortunately it also usually coincides with the limitations described above; the kind of conditions, in fact, in which it is highly unlikely that anyone will be aware that the unplanned moving of very young children to inadequate foster homes is infinitely more damaging than the sexual abuse to which they have been subjected.

The diminishing social-work role

The most serious criticism in the Cleveland report is that social-services management did not concern itself with these wider and crucial issues of categorization and family and social contexts. This is a criticism that can be made of very many other authorities. The consequence of this, of course, as underlined repeatedly in the report, was to bestow upon the paediatrician an authority and influence totally unwarranted. Social workers throughout the country will not have failed to notice the increasing domination of the case-conference phase of child sexual-abuse work by paediatricians in particular. That is not the fault of paediatricians; it stems entirely from social workers' own lack of confidence about the value of their own assessment. This is the reason for the indifferent or cynical lack of preparation by social workers; their inability to articulate on crucial areas that are very much their own domain. It is ironical and depressing to watch social workers who have not even provided a report for the conference, stuttering and stammering their way through topics on which they should be providing the most systematic, detailed and coherent observations. It is a matter of much regret that their team leader/supervisor sits idly by and may not see anything wrong with that contribution. This process of encroachment by other professionals and the corresponding timidity of management has to be reversed without any disrespect or undermining of the multi-disciplinary effort (many paediatricians and police officers would now wish that social workers would have been far more assertive in their contributions!). Fortunately that reversal is well under way, and its successful completion will ensure that the case conference assumes once again the significance that it warrants: it is the necessary and logical conclusion to the referral, investigative and intervention phases. The quality of its discussion and decision-making will be

determined by the appropriateness and effectiveness of social-work actions
in particular, taken throughout those three preceding phases.

Summary and conclusions

A particular category of child sexual-abuse case has been identified as the
one likely to pose the greatest challenge to professionals attempting to
protect and serve the best interests of the child. The child is aged
approximately between the ages of two and seven. The perpetrator is his or
her father or stepfather, and the abuse is likely to be manual and oral
masturbation, digital penetration, and other peripheral acts of manipulation
and gratification on the part of the perpetrator. Faced with a deluge of child
sexual-abuse referrals, social-services departments have not yet had time to
evolve a coherent philosophy, formulate sensible and well-tested policies, or
plan effective strategies for child sexual abuse generally, or for any category
in particular. The first step is to provide a comprehensive and humane
philosophical base. Upon this base must be re-established the framework of
response that has served social workers so well in child-abuse work
generally, namely, the referral, investigation, intervention, and case
conference phases. Each of these phases necessitates comprehensive
planning and procedures, based upon the main features of the identified
category of case to which they will be applied. This framework of the four
phases has been greatly undermined by the prominence given to disclosure
work in child sexual abuse. The preoccupation with disclosure work has had
disastrous consequences upon the management of cases, and no real
progress can be made until 'disclosure' is relegated to a less prominent place
amongst the myriad of far more demanding and complex tasks. Referral,
investigation, intervention, and case conference phases should pervasively
explore the crucial issues of *protection*, *the family and social context*, and,
resources. This exploration will ensure a high quality of assessment on each
of these crucial issues. Actions which are based upon such an assessment are
likely to be the most appropriate actions.

There is a certain stage in the investigative phase of child sexual-abuse
work when the risk of self-destruction by the perpetrator – or something
worse – is very high. How the police and social services relate and act at this
particular point can minimize or maximize the danger. Ideally police and
social services should be implementing a joint strategy from the very outset,
based upon a common philosophy and mutually shared policies. Few
authorities have reached that level of sophistication for all phases of child
sexual-abuse work. Until they do, particular attention and great caution are
necessary for the investigative phase, when there should be the maximum
understanding and co-operation between these two key agencies.

Finally, the authority and status of case conferences has been greatly
diminished during recent years. Paediatric opinion has dominated to the

exclusion of vital contributions to be made by the social worker. Management has tolerated this growing trend, intensifying social workers' sense of helplessness generally, leading to their cynicism and lack of effort. This is a damaging process which has to be reversed. It can be, by the determined effort to impose structure and discipline throughout the three preceding phases. The value of discussion and decision-making in case conferences will depend entirely upon the quality of referral taking, investigation, and intervention. All of these phases of child sexual-abuse work are in effect an assessment of and response to the crucial issues of protection, family and social context and resources. The social worker is ideally placed and capable of making that assessment and response.

9
Fostering sexually abused children

Introduction

Whatever the degree of success in avoiding the abrupt and damaging removal of sexually abused children from their homes, social workers will on occasions still have to remove children. They will invariably seek foster parents to care for them and will hope that their department has invested sufficient effort, money and time in recruiting the appropriate persons to do the job effectively; foster parents for their part – particularly the most inexperienced – will rightly expect on-going training and support. This chapter aims to provide a brief but intensive training course for foster parents. The chapter will begin with some observations of the Cleveland report's perspective on the role of foster parents. It will then make some general comment about foster parents' experiences in recent years, trying to cope with the dramatic increase in the number of sexually abused and very demanding children placed with them. It will then provide a detailed step-by-step guide on planning a training programme, establishing the aims and objectives, deciding upon the composition, content and methodology, duration and location. The potential contribution of foster parents to the welfare of sexually abused children removed from their own homes cannot be overestimated. Child sexual-abuse literature therefore is hardly credible without substantial focus on the challenges which they face, and a sincere attempt to explore how best to enable them to meet those challenges.

Listening to foster parents

The Cleveland report (Butler-Sloss 1988) exposed the pressure to which many foster parents were unwillingly subjected in the spring and early summer of 1987. The principal officer concerned commented: 'The situation was untenable; we had reached the level of looking for beds for children, rather than placing children appropriately' (p. 62). This led to a number of dangerous practices: newly approved foster parents being asked to care for seriously sexually abused children suddenly removed from their parents; asking experienced foster parents to care for more children that they were registered to care for; the total lack of matching between the child's needs and what the foster parent had to offer. These pressures upon foster parents, however, were not confined to Cleveland. They were experienced by foster parents and unwilling social workers throughout the country. It is ironical that, whilst Cleveland demonstrates that it was foster parents more than any other group which bore the consequences of the unfolding tragedy, there is not a single mention of foster parents in the lengthy conclusions and recommendations of the report. Children, parents, social workers, police officers, doctors, and managers, are all the subject of wise counsel and specific recommendations, but not foster parents.

The lack of training for foster parents has often been raised in social-work journals, and in the foster parents' own publication, *Adoption and Fostering*, both before, during and after Cleveland (e.g. Blumler *et al.* 1987; Roberts 1987). Bearing in mind the facts that social workers themselves were appallingly ill-prepared for child sexual-abuse work, and that their managers had neither philosophy, policy nor strategy for coping with it, it is easy to see the limitation of social workers' usefulness to foster parents who were repeatedly seeking guidance from them on the problems of coping with sexually abused children. Foster parents expected more from the departments which employed them, and more often than not managers and social workers were unable to give any more. Consequently relationships between foster parents and social workers deteriorated considerably, and the quality and reliability of care was inevitably affected.

Underlying the pressures and the tensions created by the increase in child sexual-abuse cases, the most basic need of foster parents is for social workers to *listen* to them, and to be as frank and as honest with them as they can. This is particularly important in the matter of offering foster parents training. Foster parents are likely to know better than anybody else what they need to learn, and what skills they need to acquire. Social workers and their training departments know better than anybody else the limits of the knowledge and skill they can impart to foster parents. Here then is the first major exercise in constructing a relevant and effective training course; an intensive exploration of foster parents' perceptions of their own needs and a rigorous and honest assessment on the part of social workers and trainers of the degree to which those needs can be met. What are foster parents' perceptions of their own needs in fostering sexually abused children? What are their major concerns for which a training course may be necessary and useful? The following are the difficulties experienced by one particular group of foster parents, and repeatedly mentioned throughout a series of meetings which preceded training:

1 Being overwhelmed by the numbers and the types of child sexual-abuse cases brought to their attention.
2 Varying degrees of inhibition and fear in fostering certain sexually abused children.
3 Being unsupported by the department and/or being 'supported' by social workers as inexperienced and unknowledgeable about child sexual abuse as most foster parents are themselves.
4 Being frightened about the possibility of being accused of sexually abusing the child they foster, coupled with a persistent demand for departmental procedures which would at least let them know the course of events, if such an accusation occurred.
5 Having strong feelings of revulsion and hatred for the perpetrator of child sexual abuse.
6 Being unable to cope with the return of children to those who have sexually abused them.
7 Having no clear guidelines about the nature and extent of their work with sexually abused children, e.g. should they be involved in play therapy, or in disclosure work; should they learn how to use anatomical dolls? should they be working more closely with professionals?
8 Being worried about the impact of sexually abused children upon their own children.

Some essential components in foster-parent training

These are not in order of priority, nor can they be said to represent the views of all foster parents. What can be said with confidence however, is that some of them definitely will represent the views of the vast majority of foster parents. Numbers 5 and 6, for example, are universally shared by foster parents and should not surprise anyone who has already encountered the age-old problem of the relationships between foster parents and natural parents in child-abuse cases generally. Child sexual abuse has merely intensified that problem, and foster parents are quite capable of unwittingly (or willingly with the best intentions) creating major obstacles in the way of social workers who may be trying to rehabilitate a child to go back to his or her family of origin. A training package which did not have a component concentrating on ways of overcoming this most common problem is hardly relevant.

There are a number of interesting features about this list of difficulties. First, there is a 'mundaneness' and a 'simplicity' about them, a distinctly non-intellectual view governed by feeling and gut instinct. Second, there is not the slightest hint of foster parents wanting to know anything about one of the most dominant topics in the literature on child sexual abuse, namely, the causes of such abuse. This is eminently wise of foster parents, as the theoretical causes are very often irrelevant to the problems on hand; foster parents know it to be so. Third, there is the clear indication of foster parents' awareness of the myriad of categories of child sexual abuse cases. They are alert to the question of categorization long before trainers and practitioners are, for the simple reason that in caring for differing categories of sexually abused children twenty-four hours each day, they quickly observe the differences in the behaviour of those children, differences in their relationships with the abusing/non-abusing parents, and differences in the challenges they pose to foster families as a whole.

There is ample advice here in all of these points. For example, there is little need for the traditional practice of devoting a large chunk of the training package to the topic of 'the causes of child sexual abuse'. One group of trainers went so far as to enlighten foster parents about five different perspectives on the origins of child sexual abuse, and then 'showed foster parents that it was possible to synthesise these perspectives' (Pringle 1988: 29). This is the stuff of the academic and the professional; it is hardly what foster parents expect or need. Second, there definitely is a need to spend time on the categorization of child sexual abuse, and on exploring the impact of different categories upon the fostering family as a whole. Third, there is no justification for thinking that foster parents might benefit from any of the sexual-awareness exercises which are a standard component in the training of social workers, or, more specifically, from delving into their own childhoods in search of sexual experiences and their impacts. These are nothing more than pseudo-intellectual indulgences of dubious worth, concocted in the sparsity of knowledge and imagination about infinitely more challenging complexities and practicalities in caring for sexually abused children. Foster parents would see through them immediately. Finally, the crisis nature of child sexual abuse work (hinted at in no. 1, above) dictates the necessity of including a component in training that re-establishes basic minimum standards of practice when abused children are placed with foster parents in crisis situations. This is in effect a training in assertiveness for foster parents, many of whom have tolerated abysmal standards of practice by social workers placing sexually abused children with them. Needless to say, social workers themselves may benefit enormously from such a training!

Let us then proceed with a choice of topics more clearly defined, and decide on what the aims and objectives of the course will be.

Aims and objectives

Knowledge, awareness, skills

Few foster parents have time for training (a reality long recognized by management who sensibly do not make training compulsory), and few foster parents have had any additional training to that which they received during their application for registration. These two probabilities have enormous implications for offering foster parents training in the most complex and challenging field of child sexual abuse. First, they dictate the duration of the course which, realistically, cannot be more than a few days or half a dozen evenings spread over a period of weeks. Second, they dictate an emphasis upon increasing knowledge and enhancing awareness rather than upon the much more complicated and time-consuming task of teaching skills and techniques. Skills and techniques can be acquired through various means, and at a later stage; what foster parents initially require are knowledge and increased awareness of the specific topics they repeatedly bring to social workers' attention. Whatever the statement of aims and objectives, however, the language in which it is conveyed is crucial. Some poor advertising about fostering gives the impression that all foster parents are educated, articulate, socially sophisticated people. Fortunately they are not, more often (in my experience) residing in locations seldom far from where the children they care for originate; familiar with poverty and unemployment, encountering all kinds of communication difficulties with social services and other agencies. 'Synthesizing perspectives on child sexual abuse' is not the language of the vast majority of foster parents; nor for that matter is the 'categorization of child sexual abuse'. Bearing this in mind, the aims and objectives deriving from the above discussion may be formally conveyed to foster parents as follows:

The broad aims
1 To explore many of the difficult areas of fostering sexually abused children which you have repeatedly brought to our attention.
2 To learn about and to be more aware of the causes of the difficulties you encounter.
3 To increase confidence in coping with these difficulties.

The specific objectives
1 To look at the huge range of child sexual-abuse offences, and to explore some of the differences between these offences.
2 To look at the many different ages of children who are sexually abused. We will discuss the question: which children, and what type of abuse have you found the most challenging, and why?
3 To seek out the right kind of atmosphere in a foster home for different age groups, for different types of abuse.
4 To explore the impact of the abused child upon your own family; to ask: how can we minimize any bad impact?
5 To discuss child sexual abusers; to look at different types of abusers and the offences they commit; to explore our own feelings towards them; to ask how these offenders affect the task we have of caring for their victims.
6 To learn about departmental procedures whenever foster parents are accused of sexually abusing the fostered child.
7 To restate and reassert the basic minimum standards of service which foster parents need from social workers and the department when sexually abused children are placed with them.

Course leaders

In the relatively new field of child sexual abuse, there is an understandable tendency to rely upon reputed experts from outside one's own department for most types of training provision. This may not be sensible in training foster parents. Their problems stem from the department which employs them; the department's resources or lack of them, the relationships between the department's personnel and themselves, their general perceptions of the department and the service it provides for them. Problems also stem from the cultural and environmental features in the foster parents' own lives; their own localities and families; and from the known characteristics of the child sexual-abuse problem in their own and the department's area. Outside speakers/trainers, no matter how expert and knowledgeable, simply won't address most of these problems, for the even more simple reason that they are unlikely to know anything about them. Their expertise is often a pleasant and convenient diversion from the many problems that foster parents and social workers will face all over again when the outsiders have gone. For this reason, I favour training initiatives created and implemented by fostering and other personnel within the department, particularly those who have been doing the most *listening* to and working with foster parents. There should, of course, be opportunities for guest speakers at certain stages in the training, in which their knowledge and expertise in specific and common problem areas will be most welcome, e.g. communicating with sexually abused toddlers, working with perpetrators, etc. And there should be no hesitation in seeking advice and help from the department's training section. (I have nearly always found the training section's experience and participation to be invaluable.)

A slight practical problem

The problem with offering foster parents any kind of training about sexually abused children is that we have placed with them sexually abused children so demanding that they don't have any time for training! Unless the department is going to subsidize fully and/or provide comprehensive crèche and child-minding facilities, or unless such facilities can be got elsewhere, forget about training foster parents. In my last training initiative with foster parents, we had to employ four adults, aided by three volunteers, to care for twenty-nine children!

Number and composition

There are numerous and valuable texts which address the issues of a suitable composition and number for training-group initiatives. However, the problems of fostering sexually abused children and the reality of the variations in the fostering scenes throughout the country necessitate some additional considerations. I have worked in rural areas where it would have been impossible to get more than half a dozen foster parents attending anything provided by the department. I have also worked in inner-city areas where fifty or more foster parents live within the same square mile. Obviously the latter is very convenient for both course leaders and foster parents; it offers the opportunity of seeking viable numbers and ideal composition. My own experience leads me to believe that three course leaders and approximately twenty foster parents is a reasonable ratio; it provides for a sense of security in numbers which foster parents will very much appreciate in the initial stages of the training, and it also facilitates the ideal 1:7 ratio for small group exercises and discussions.

The composition of the course leaders' group is just as important as that of the foster parents. There should be significant differences in the personalities, styles and attitudes; there should be a male/female mix; there should be the highest level of harmony and compatibility despite any conspicuous differences in outlook or convictions. The composition of the foster parents' group is not always subject to choice. But the usual principle of avoiding dominating individuals or subgroups is vitally important in an area of discussion that is so potentially inhibiting. Fostering *couples* are preferable to the common tendency for mothers only to turn up, and an all out effort should be made to convince fathers about the worth of the course. This preference should not, however, preclude the attendance of the increasing number of single parents who are now fostering (and who, in my experience, demonstrate a commitment, enthusiasm and quality of fostering that few couples can better).

Duration and location

Many foster parents regularly attend support-group meetings. These last a certain length of time, take place in a certain location and generate a certain relaxing, familiar atmosphere. Duration, location and the atmosphere of a training course on fostering sexually abused children should be conspicuously different, underlining the fact that it is far more than a mere support-group meeting. Duration, location and atmosphere will undoubtedly be dictated by practical considerations, as they are for support-group meetings, but there is a need for much more formality, structure and discipline in training. Thus an entirely different location is desirable, equipped with basic educational aids. It has already been suggested that the duration of an intensive training course is unlikely to be more than three days (lucky the foster parents who can afford three full days) or half a dozen evenings. In fact, a mix is preferable, with one whole day to start with (usually a Saturday), followed by three, four or five evenings, one per week. Whether day or evening, training sessions should be no longer than three hours, with at least one generous break in the middle.

Method

The usual ways and means of achieving aims and objectives in any training course are appropriate here: formal lecture by one or more course leaders, followed by question-and-answer session, debate and argument; small group discussions; small group exercises; role play; training cassettes, guest speakers; home exercises, etc. It is very important to explore carefully the possibility of each of these, to explore both their potential and their danger (for example, asking foster parents to role-play sexually abusing situations within a family is fraught with risk). The choice will best be made by those who know their foster parents best, one of the reasons for preferring course leaders from within the department to those from outside.

Whatever the methodology, the course material, i.e. case histories, specific child sexual-abuse problems, should always be sought from the foster-parent perspective. For example, if one is asking foster parents to be considering a number of child sexual-abuse problems, the child at the centre of each of those problems should be in a fostering situation: 'the child you are fostering . . .'; 'the mother (or father) of the child you are fostering . . .', etc.

Introductions

The usual preliminaries and introductions should be dominated by assurances to the foster parents that they are not going to be exposed. Many ill-prepared discussions in training for child sexual-abuse work have been devastating for participants suddenly overwhelmed by memories of their own or their loved one's experiences. Foster parents should be cautioned at the outset that that is always a possibility, but that the content and boundaries of each component of the course will be spelt out before commencement and, if they anticipate such a possibility, they can withdraw at that early stage. If it is the intention of the course leaders to use role play, particularly with video recording, then reassurances about not being exposed are doubly necessary. Another task in this introductory session is to emphasize that the course content has been determined by foster parents themselves; some memories of particular foster parents harping on about not knowing this and that is an effective and light-hearted way of getting the point across; it gives the course additional status and commands more respect and commitment.

Session 1: The range of child sexual-abuse offences

This is essentially an exercise with an identical objective to that of nearly every chapter in this book, namely, to enable and to encourage foster parents to discriminate throughout the whole field of child sexual abuse.

Table 9.1   Classifying child sexual abuse

Sex of child	Age of child	Type of abuse	Who is the perpetrator or alleged perpetrator?	Parents' reaction	When and/or where the abuse was committed?
Male	0– 2	flashing/ exposure	father	shock/ horror	one isolated incident of abuse recently
Female	3– 5		mother	anger	a series of sexual abuses completed over a long time
	6– 8	pornography (magazines, photographs, videos)	step-father stepmother	disbelief	sexual abuse committed by numerous perpetrators over a long time
	9–11	inappropriate touching	brother/ sister	guilt/ remorse	when parents were present
	12–16	oral sex	uncle/aunt	denial	when parents were absent
		buggery	grandfather	disowning	abuse in home
		intercourse (non-incestuous)	grandmother	comforting	abuse in relatives' home
		intercourse (incestuous)	neighbour	accusing	abuse in neighbours' home
		rape	childminder		abuse in school
		post-natal maternal incest	foster parent		abuse in residential home
					abuse in foster home

There is, of course, the additional objective of exploring the implications of that categorizing process for foster parents.

What do foster parents already know about the range of offences? Ask them to name the offence committed against the child they are at present fostering. There are likely to be two contrasting responses: first, many offences will be revealed; second, some foster parents will not know what offences have been committed against their foster child, a not unusual lapse on the part of the social worker who has placed the child. The first objective here is getting foster parents to accept that it is absolutely essential for them to seek as much information as possible about the abuse, the circumstances surrounding it, the identity of the perpetrator, and details about the family of the child. Many instances of the consequences of not knowing, for the quality of care and the interactions with the child, should be provided. The second objective is to ensure that foster parents adopt a permanently discriminating attitude (much easier with foster parents than with social workers, as the former are being constantly made to think differently about different categories of sexually abused children, because of the different challenges they pose).

Table 9.1 encompasses many of the categories and circumstances of abuse. Having had the opportunity to study it, foster parents should be asked which particular set of circumstance is most relevant or important to them: is it the sex or age of the child? the type of abuse they have suffered? the identity of the perpetrator? the reaction of the parents? the location or time in which the offence was committed? The reasons why foster parents believe one set of circumstances is more important than another should be elicited; shared experiences, perceptions and themes will then emerge; and debate about how foster parents have responded in the past to these. For example, various initial disjointed responses may be saying something about foster parents' wariness in taking a child who seems to be acting out many of the experiences to which he or she has been subjected. Subtle leading is likely, however, to clarify the real problem: that foster fathers in particular are very apprehensive of sexually abused, four-to-five-year-old girls whose behaviour is disgustingly sexualized. If this can be identified as a problem, the analysis and possible solution are an excellent topic for small group discussion. Course leaders, however, should be aware of some risks: that foster fathers, for example, will immediately recognize their own vulnerability in cases like these and yet may feel hypocritical or dishonest or cowardly in not being able to say so. (See table 8.1.)

Session 2: Creating the right kind of atmosphere for sexually abused children

Foster parents will want to know a lot more than is obvious in this title. The right atmosphere for whom? what? when? There are three major questions underlying this topic:

1 What kind of atmosphere and response from foster parents is most appropriate when a sexually abused child is placed with them?
2 Should foster parents be involved in disclosure work? and if so, how best can they facilitate it?
3 How can foster parents best contribute to the child's recovery from the effects of the abuse and, more importantly, from the often greater trauma of removal from his or her family?

Even without the tentative categorization efforts in session 1, foster parents will very quickly enquire what child we are referring to in each of these questions. Therein lies another exercise: for foster parents themselves to choose a particular category or categories of sexually abused children for whom the matter of 'the right atmosphere' is vitally important in each of the above three stages. All discussion should be supplemented with the additional enquiry: for what child, out of what circumstances, is it most difficult for foster parents to provide the right atmosphere, and why?

These are vastly open-ended questions, with literally hundreds of answers. The course leaders should begin by emphasizing the point that there are no experts who can answer on behalf of every sexually abused child. A sensible way forward is to concentrate on a limited number of categories of abused children. A list of examples of fostering placements, one from each category, should be made out. The foster parents should be asked to imagine each of these children arriving at their home with the social worker. Substantial details should be given about each case. The three questions above can then be addressed. Again, out of an initial chaos of responses will emerge common difficulties experienced, and themes and patterns more easily grasped. There will be cases in which foster parents display great insight, patience, tolerance, fortitude and effectiveness; but there will be other cases where there will be a collective sigh of exasperation, and they will admit that the case is too difficult or dangerous for them. One such example I recall was that of a twelve-year-old boy, repeatedly buggered by his father. When the abuse was exposed, the boy was removed immediately to a foster home, his mother walked out on her husband, and he persistently denied abusing his son. On the same day, the husband went after his wife, strangled her and then hung himself. As we have seen in previous chapters, murders and suicides are not uncommonly linked with child sexual abuse, providing a sound reason for using this kind of example in such an exercise. However, foster parents can be assured that they are not supposed to be miracle workers. They should be reminded that there isn't a foster parent, social worker, psychiatrist anywhere in the country that would know precisely how to care for this particular child. That in itself is a major step forward, as it means that the full horror of this child's situation is fully realized, and that major trauma and long-term effects are predictable. It will also rid foster parents of any illusions they may have that their own efforts and dedication will suffice in enabling the child to integrate easily into their family.

Some foster parents have not been able to resist, indeed, have been encouraged by some social workers, to attempt to get disclosures from children. There is a need for a clear policy statement forbidding such dangerous practice. However, foster parents, by virtue of the stability, security and trust which they bring into the lives of sexually abused children, can often find themselves in a situation in which a child, particularly an adolescent, will feel that it is safe to disclose whatever has happened to them. An exercise in which such a situation is imagined or, better still, is role played, with an experienced outsider acting the part of the child, will be highly productive in terms of arriving at a consensus as to the most appropriate responses by the listening foster parent.

One final point on the foster parents' contribution to the long-term rehabilitation of sexually abused children. An audience of social workers and managers might be more appropriate, as they will undoubtedly hear foster parents justifiably complain that they are denied information about the department's planning for children, about the current state of circumstances within the child's family and that they are excluded from therapy and counselling the child may be receiving outside the home (e.g. in a hospital, school, clinic or social-services office). This is gross negligence on the part of the social worker, and any therapeutic or counselling effort will be futile if the principal carer of the child is not at least aware of and supportive of it, better still, is an active part of it. This point will emerge again in the session dealing with foster parents' assertiveness.

Session 3: The impact of sexually abused children upon the fostering family

This may be the most difficult session. Foster parents are often deeply moved by the suffering and degradation endured by sexually abused children. They will often make any effort or sacrifice on behalf of such children. But the impact of that child upon the relationships between the foster mother and father and upon the fostering family as a whole may be devastating. Experienced social workers will recall many instances when foster parents have rung them demanding that they remove the child immediately 'before our family falls apart . . .' or 'before either one of us walks out!' Because of the exceptional difficulties posed by the behaviour of certain categories of sexually abused children, these instances are likely to have increased in recent years. The problem, however, is not new: foster parents are reluctant to inform social workers that they are having difficulty with any placement; they can often feel guilty and inadequate if they are; they may fear the removal of the child if they do inform the social worker. Even now, in a training session dealing specifically with all these issues, foster parents may still be loath to acknowledge the problem; I can recall a session like this, attended by numerous foster parents who had experienced major crises within their families because of the impact made by the sexually abused child; yet despite gentle, sensitive probing, they could not share these experiences with the other participants.

This session, therefore, has three related exercises: first, to explore the nature and extent of the impact of sexually abused children upon fostering families; second, to examine the deteriorating processes which inevitably lead to that ultimatum to the social worker to get the child removed; third, to explore the reasons why foster parents do not at any stage during those deteriorating processes seek advice, help and support from the department.

There are two major objectives throughout these exercises: to enhance foster parents' awareness of the less obvious impact of the placement, demonstrating the normality and inevitability of that impact, and to remove the perceptual and other obstacles which stand in the way of foster parents sharing their experiences with the social worker.

Session 4: Child sexual abusers

There will be no reluctance on the part of foster parents to express their views and feelings about perpetrators. This session requires extra special planning and discipline, if it is not to be sabotaged by pervasive hostility and anger, directed at both the perpetrators and the social-services department that has anything to do with them. The strongest feelings are reserved for social workers who would dare try to rehabilitate and return a child to the man who has sexually abused that child.

The underlying problem is once again the lack of discrimination in thought and attitude towards perpetrators. This can be borne out by a simple, light-hearted exercise, asking foster parents to construct a profile of 'the typical perpetrator'. A common perception is that of the bald-headed, ugly, middle-aged stranger, slimy and greasy, perpetrating diabolical acts against very young children, and all this despite the fact that they know the abuser of the children they are fostering bears no resemblance at all to this profile.

A second exercise will quickly get foster parents to the core of this problem and solve it at the same time. A list of perpetrators and details of their offences and relationship with their victims can be circulated. These offences should range from the least serious (e.g. a single-parent father committing a single act of abuse, trying to get into the bed of his teenage daughter after a few drinks, admitting the offence, feeling deeply ashamed and remorseful about it, and apologizing to his daughter) to the most serious (e.g. a twenty-five-year-old uncle repeatedly buggering and raping the children of his sister, whilst minding them). Between these extremes, there should be about six other offences of varying degrees of seriousness. Foster parents should then be asked to list them in terms of seriousness, i.e. the short- and long-term impact of the abuse upon the victims.

Some unpalatable experiences emerge from this exercise: first, foster parents actually expose their inability to discriminate between entirely different, unrelated offences. The difference between the above two perpetrators, for example, is so great that foster parents will realize the inappropriateness of applying the term 'child sexual abuse' to both of them. Second, these offences will be a topic for discussion in the small-group exercises; some foster fathers will actually admit then that it would not be too difficult to commit such an offence themselves. In either case, this exercise will have a profound effect upon foster parents, particularly foster fathers, and is likely to modify their views and feelings on the topic significantly.

Another exercise in this session is to enhance awareness of the fact that perpetrators may be enormously important to the child they have abused and may be deeply respected by that child. This again is difficult for foster parents to accept, particularly for those foster parents who declare at the outset that they never want to meet a perpetrator and will not contemplate one being present in their home. But it is not difficult to elicit from foster parents the acknowledgement that it is the children themselves who repeatedly remind us of how much some perpetrators have contributed to other aspects of the abused child's life. The ultimate objective is for foster parents to be more aware of the damage they may be doing to the fostered child merely by harbouring these intense feelings of hostility towards perpetrators. A final exercise is appropriate, in which such cases can be identified, and illustrations given of how these feelings will almost certainly adversely affect the quality of the care which they provide.

Session 5: Foster parents accused of sexually abusing the fostered child

It is not uncommon for foster parents to be accused of abusing a child and to be subjected to a traumatic investigation by the department which employs them (Nixon *et al.* 1986). Authorities are increasingly addressing the problem and producing policy and detailed procedures to guide workers through this most unwelcome task. If such procedures are available, this session should examine them. It is unlikely that the impact of an investigation can be minimized; it is and always will be a devastating experience; but familiarity with the procedures and role playing of an actual investigation will ensure that foster parents do not suffer the additional trauma caused by: 'I never thought this could happen to me.' There is no substitute for carefully worked out procedures consistently applied in all such investigations. Every foster parent should have a copy of these procedures. In authorities which don't have any, and which rely on crisis management at the time an allegation against a foster parent is made, the value of a training session on this issue will be greatly minimized.

Session 6: The needs of foster parents when a sexually abused child is placed

Foster parents have given social workers the benefit of the doubt in the recent upsurge in placements of sexually abused children. They recognized that social workers were overwhelmed by the increase in the detection of the abuse, the demands for the removal of children, and in the often frantic search for placement at any hour of the day. Just as social-work standards in referral-taking, investigation, intervention and case conferences, were lowered quite drastically as a consequence of the increase, so too did the necessary standards of practice in placing abused children. It is now time for foster parents to reassert basic minimum standards, in the interests of social workers as much as for themselves but, more importantly, in the interests of the child. Course leaders should not view this session as potentially disloyal to their own employer; foster parents are employees too, the most valuable child-care resource the department has.

Social-services departments will already have placement procedures. These should be reviewed in the light of the dramatic increase in placing sexually abused children. Are there any additions or modifications necessary specifically for sexually abused children? The role playing of such a placement will be particularly productive (as well as giving foster parents a much needed bit of fun in acting out just how badly some children have been placed with them). Planning, preparing both child and foster parents, carrying out the placement with the least possible haste, and informing foster parents of all available information about the child are all essential ingredients in the return to basic minimum standards.

Session 7: The fostering of children who have AIDS

This is one session that was not included in the formal agenda, simply because it is one that foster parents are not likely to want. (I write from experience of trying to find a placement for a child strongly suspected of having the AIDS virus). Whether such a session is included or not, there is a paramount need for educating foster parents and social workers in preparation for the inevitability of a dramatic increase in the placement of children who have been sexually abused by the carriers of the AIDS virus, or by those who have been diagnosed as HIV positive. The British Agencies for Adoption and Fostering (BAAF) have produced a valuable text on the topic, entitled, *The Implications of AIDS for Children in Care* (1987). In the absence of literature based upon extensive experience of the problem (as in Edinburgh, for example), BAAF's text provides a basis for an introductory course on the topic.

Summary and conclusions

Foster parents have often been recognized as the most valuable child-care resource outside the family, yet they have been largely ignored in the recent crises associated with child sexual abuse, when social-services departments depended upon them so much. Foster parents too need training and preparation for working with and caring for sexually abused children. They are well qualified, through hard experience, to say what kind of training they need, to identify the areas most challenging to them, and to seek understanding about the behaviour of social workers and managers which may, in respect of child sexual-abuse cases, be inexplicable to them. Any training provision for foster parents should be based upon an intensive listening and consultative process on the part of social workers. Social services cannot offer a comprehensive training package covering all problems encountered in fostering sexually abused children, but it certainly can aim to enhance foster parents' awareness and understanding in certain key areas. The specific objectives should be determined largely by foster parents themselves or, if that is unacceptable, then at least there should be foster-parent representation on whichever body is so deciding. Training-course leaders should be familiar with the foster parents and with all the problems arising in the working relationships between foster parents and the departments in the whole area of child sexual abuse. There should be diversity of interest, gender and personality amongst course leaders, and a reasonable cross-section of foster parents which excludes domineering individuals or cliques. Duration, location and atmosphere may be dictated by practical considerations, but should also aim at enhancing the status of the course, by differentiating it from other provisions for foster parents, e.g. support groups, social events, etc.

All training should be evaluated. But the usual practice of asking course participants to complete a questionnaire immediately on finishing the course should be avoided. Foster parents should be consulted some time after the course, no less than six weeks, and then asked to discuss the impact of any part of the course upon their fostering of sexually abused children in the intervening time. A questionnaire covering all aspects of the course, and specifically addressing the original aims and objectives, should then be distributed, to be completed at the foster parents' convenience.

Bibliography

Bagley, C. and Ramsay, R. (1987). 'Disrupted childhood and vulnerability to sexual assault: long term sequels with implications for counselling', referred to in D. Finkelhor (1986). *A Source Book on Child Sexual Abuse*. Beverly Hills, CA, Sage.

Baker, A. and Duncan, S. (1985). 'Child sexual abuse: a study of prevalence in Great Britain'. *Child Abuse and Neglect*, 9, 457–67.

Barker, P. (1982). *Union Street*. London, Virago.

Batty, D. (ed.) (1987). *The Implications of AIDS for Children in Care*. London, British Agencies for Adoption and Fostering.

Bentovim, A. (1987). 'Physical and sexual abuse of children: the role of the family therapist'. *Journal of Family Therapy*, 9 (4), 383–8.

Bentovim, A. (1988). 'Who is to blame?'. *New Statesman and Society*, 5 August 1988, 29.

Benward, J. and Densen-Gerber, J. (1979). 'Incest as a causative factor in anti-social behaviour: an exploratory study'. *Contemporary Drug Problems*, 4 (3), 323–39.

Berliner, L. and Stevens, D. (1982). 'Clinical issues in child sexual abuse'. *Journal of Social Work and Human Sexuality*, vols. 1 and 2, 93–108.

Biestik, F. (1961). *The Casework Relationship*. London, Unwin.

Blom-Cooper, L. (1985). *A Child In Trust: Report of the Panel of Enquiry into Circumstances Surrounding the Death of Jasmine Beckford*. Brent Borough Council.

Blumler, J., Keyte, M. and Wiles, A. (1987). 'Training foster parents about sexual abuse'. *Adoption and Fostering*, 11 (2), 32–4.

Boushel, M. and Noakes, S. (1988). 'Islington Social Services: developing a policy on child sexual abuse'. *Feminist Review*, 28, 150–7.

Bowlby, J. (1988). 'The Bowlby interview'. *Association of Family Therapy Newsletter*, 7 (2), 6–11.

Briere, J. (1984). 'The long-term effects of childhood sexual abuse: defining a past sexual abuse syndrome'. Paper presented at the 3rd National Conference on

Sexual Victimization of Children, Washington DC, quoted in Finkelhor, D. (1986). *A Source Book on Child Sexual Abuse.* Beverly Hills, CA, Sage.

British Association of Social Workers (1988). *A Code of Ethics for Social Workers.*

Burgess, A. W. and Holstrom, L. L. (1974). 'Rape trauma syndrome'. *American Journal of Psychiatry,* 131 (9), 981–6.

Burgess, A. W. and Holstrom, L. L. (1979). *Rape: Crisis and Recovery.* Maryland, Bardy.

Burgess, A. W., Groth, A. N. and McCauseland, M. P. (1981). 'Child sex initiation rings'. *American Journal of Orthopsychiatry,* 51 (1), 110–19.

Burnam, A. (1985). 'Personal communication concerning the Los Angeles epidemiological catchment area study', quoted in Finkelhor, D. (1986). *A Source Book on Child Sexual Abuse.* Beverly Hills, CA, Sage.

Butler-Sloss, E. (1988). *Report of the Enquiry into Child Abuse in Cleveland, 1987.* London, HMSO.

Cavallin, H. (1966). 'Incestuous fathers: a clinical report'. *American Journal of Psychiatry,* 122 (10), 1132–8.

Chandler, S. M. (1982). 'Knowns and unknowns in sexual abuse of children'. *Journal of Social Work and Human Sexuality,* vols. 1 and 2, 51–68.

Chasnoff, M. D., Burns, W. J., Scholl, S. H., Burns, K., Chisum, G. and Kyle-Spore, L. (1986). 'Maternal neo-natal incest'. *American Journal of Orthopsychiatry,* 56 (4), 577–80.

'Childwatch' (1986). BBC 1, 30 October 1986.

CIBA Foundation (1984). *Child Sexual Abuse Within the Family.* London, Tavistock.

Conte, J. R. (1982). 'Sexual abuse of children: enduring issues for social work'. *Journal of Social Work and Human Sexuality,* vols. 1 and 2, 1–19.

Corby, B. (1987). *Working With Child Abuse.* Milton Keynes, Open University Press.

Coveney, L., Jackson, M., Jeffries, S., Kaye, L. and Mahoney, P. (1984). *The Sexuality Papers: Male Sexuality and the Social Control of Women.* London, Hutchinson.

Dale, P. (1987). Letter to Editor of *Community Care,* 26 November 1987.

Dale, P., Waters, J., Davies, M., Roberts, W. and Morrison, T. (1986a). 'The tower of silence: creative and destructive issues for therapeutic teams dealing with sexual abuse'. *Journal of Family Therapy,* 8, 1–25.

Dale, P., Davies, M., Morrison, T. and Waters, J. (1986b). *Dangerous Families.* London, Tavistock.

DHSS (1982). *Child Abuse: A Study of Enquiry Reports, 1973–81.* London, HMSO.

De Francis, V. (1969). *Protecting the Child Victim of Sex Crimes Committed by Adults.* Denver, CO, American Humane Association.

De Mause, L. (1974). *The History of Childhood.* New York, Psychohistory Press.

De Young, M. (1986). 'A conceptual model for judging the truthfulness of a young child's allegation of sexual abuse'. *American Journal of Orthopsychiatry,* 56 (4), 550–9.

Devereaux, G. (1939). 'The social and cultural implications of incest among the Mohave Indians'. *Psychoanalysis,* 8, 510–23.

Eldridge, H. and Gibbs, P. (1987). 'Strategies for preventing reoffending: a course for sex offenders'. *Probation Journal,* 34, no. 1, 7–9.

Ennew, J. (1986). *The Sexual Exploitation of Children.* Cambridge, Polity Press.

Ethelmer, E. (1897). *Phases of Love,* referred to in Coveney, L., Jackson, M.,

Jeffries, S., Kay, L. and Mahoney, P. (1984). *The Sexuality Papers: Male Sexuality and the Social Control of Women*. London, Hutchinson.

Fawcett, M. (1892). *On the Amendments Required by the Criminal Law Amendment Act 1885*. London, Women's Printing Society.

Finkelhor, D. (1979). *Sexually Victimized Children*. New York, Free Press.

Finkelhor, D. (1984). *Child Sexual Abuse*. New York, Free Press.

Finkelhor, D. (1986). *A Source Book on Child Sexual Abuse*. Beverly Hills, CA, Sage.

Finkelhor, D. and Browne, A. (1985). 'The traumatic impact of child sexual abuse: a conceptualization'. *American Journal of Orthopsychiatry*, 55 (4), 530–41.

Fontaine, J. (1988). *Child Sexual Abuse*. London, The Economic and Social Research Council.

Fox, S. S. and Scherl, D. J. (1972). 'Crisis intervention with victims of rape'. *Social Work*, 17 (1), 37–42.

Furniss, T. (1983). 'Family process in the treatment of intra familial child sexual abuse'. *Journal of Family Therapy*, 5, 263–78.

Giarretto, H. (1978). 'Humanistic treatment of father–daughter incest'. *Journal of Humanistic Psychology*, 18 (4), 59–76.

Giarretto, H. (1981). 'A comprehensive child sexual abuse treatment programme', in Mrazek, P. B. and Kempe, C. H. (eds) (1981). *Sexually Abused Children and their Families*. Oxford, Pergamon, 179–98.

Glaser, D. and Frosh, S. (1988). *Child Sexual Abuse*. London, Macmillan.

Goodwin, J., Simms, M. and Bergman, R. (1979). 'Hysterical seizures: a sequel to incest'. *American Journal of Orthopsychiatry*, 49 (4), 698–703.

Goodwin, J., MacCarthy, T. and De Vesto, P. (1981). 'Prior incest in mothers of abused children'. *Child Abuse and Neglect*, 5, 87–96.

Groth, N. A. (1978). 'Guidelines for assessment and management of the offender', in Burgess, A., Groth, A., Holmstrom, L. and Sgroi, S. (eds). *Sexual Assault of Children and Adolescents*. Lexington, Lexington Books.

Hadley, J. (1987). 'Mum is not the word'. *Community Care*, 5 November 1987.

Hamilton, C. (1909). *Marriage as a Trade*. London, Chapman & Hall.

Herman, J. and Hirschman, L. (1977). 'Father–daughter incest'. *Signs: Journal of Women in the Culture and Society*, 2, 735–56.

Heywood, J. (1964). *Introduction to Teaching Casework Skills*. London, Routledge & Kegan Paul.

Houlihan, J. (1986). 'Permission to tell', *Community Care*, 23 October 1986.

Jackson, M. (1984). 'Sexology and the social construction of male sexuality', in Coveney, L., Jackson, M., Jeffries, S., Kay, L. and Mahony, P. (1984). *The Sexuality Papers: Male Sexuality and the Social Control of Women*. London, Hutchinson, 45–68.

James, J. and Meyerding, J. (1977). 'Early sexual experience and prostitution'. *American Journal of Psychiatry*, 134, 1381.

Jeffries, S. (1984). '"Free from all uninvited touch of man": women's campaigns around sexuality, 1880–1914' in Coveney, L., Jackson, M., Jeffries, S., Kay, L. and Mahony, P. (1984). *The Sexuality Papers: Male Sexuality and the Social Control of Women*. London, Hutchinson, 22–44.

Kaufman, I., Peck, A. L. and Tagiuri, C. R. (1954). 'The family constellation and overt incestuous relations between father and daughter'. *American Journal of Orthopsychiatry*, 24 (2), 266–79.

Kempe, R. S. and Kempe, C. H. (1978). *Child Abuse*. London, Fontana Open Books.

Kohan, M. J., Pothier, P. and Norbeck, J. S. (1987). 'Hospitalized children with a history of sexual abuse'. *American Journal of Orthopsychiatry*, 57 (2), 258–64.

Lamb, S. (1986). 'Treating sexually abused children: issues of blame and responsibility'. *American Journal of Orthopsychiatry*, 56 (2), 303–6.

Landis, J. T. (1956). 'Experience of 500 children with adult sexual deviation'. *Psychiatric Quarterly Supplement*, 30, 91–9.

Lukianowicz, N. (1972). 'Incest I: paternal incest'. *British Journal of Psychiatry*, 120, 301–13.

MacLeod, M. and Saraga, E. (1987). 'Child sexual abuse: a feminist perspective'. *Spare Rib*, July 1987, 22–6.

McFarlane, K. (1978). 'Sexual abuse of children', in Chapman, J. R. and Gates, M. (1978) (eds). *The Victimization of Women*. Beverly Hills, CA, Sage.

McFarlane, K. and Buckley, J. (1982). 'Treating child sexual abuse: an overview of current treatment models'. *Journal of Social Work and Human Sexuality*, vols 1 and 2, 69–91.

McIntyre, K. (1981). 'Role of mothers in father–daughter incest: a feminist analysis'. *Social Work*, 26 (6), 462–7.

MacLeod, M. and Saraga, E. (1988a). 'Challenging the orthodoxy: towards a feminist theory and practice'. *Feminist Review*, no. 28, 16–55.

MacLeod, M. and Saraga, E. (1988b). 'Against orthodoxy, *New Statesman and Society*, July, 1988.

Meiselman, K. (1978). *Incest: A Psychological Study of Cause and Effects with Treatment Recommendations*. San Francisco, Josey Bass.

Metropolitan Police and Bexley Social Services (1987). *Child Sexual Abuse Joint Investigative Programme, Bexley Experiment*. London, HMSO.

Minuchin, S. (1974). *Families and Family Therapy*. London, Tavistock.

Minuchin, S. and Fishman, H. C. (1981). *Family Therapy Techniques*. Cambridge, MA, Harvard University Press.

Moore, J. (1985). *The ABC of Child Abuse*. Aldershot, Gower.

Mrazek, P. B. and Mrazek, D. A. (1981). 'The effects of child sexual abuse', in Mrazek, P. B. and Kempe, C. H. (eds). *Sexually Abused Children and Their Families*. Oxford, Pergamon, p. 235–45.

Mrazek, P. B. (1981). 'Definition and recognition of sexual child abuse', in Mrazek, P. B. and Kempe, C. H. (1981) (eds). *Sexually Abused Children and their Families*, Oxford, Pergamon, 5–16.

Mrazek, P. B. (1981). 'Incest and the Dysfunctional Family System', in Mrazek, P. B. and Kempe, C. H. (eds). *Sexually Abused Children and Their Families*. Oxford, Pergamon, 167–78.

Nash, C. C. and West, D. J. (1985). 'Sexual molestation of young girls', in West, D. J. (1985) (ed.). *Sexual Victimization*. Aldershot, Gower.

National Centre on Child Abuse and Neglect (1987). *Interdisciplinary Glossary on Child Abuse and Neglect*. Washington DC, U.S. Dept. of Education, 1978.

Nixon, S., Hicks, C. and Ellis, S. (1986). 'Support for foster parents accused of child abuse'. *Foster Care*, December 1986.

O'Hagan, K. P. (1980). 'Is social work necessary?'. *Community Care*, 297, 24–6.

O'Hagan, K. P. (1986a). *Crisis Intervention in Social Services*. London, Macmillan.

O'Hagan, K. P. (1986b). 'Training for crises'. *Social Work Today*, 29 September 1986.

O'Hagan, K. P. (1988). 'A social work categorization of child sexual abuse'. *Practice*, vol. 2, 3.

Pankhurst, C. (1913). *Plain Facts About a Great Evil*. London, Women's Social and Political Union.

Panton, J. H. (1979). 'MMPI Profile configurations associated with incestuous and non-incestuous child molesting'. *Psychological Reports*, 45, 335–8.

Parker, H. and Parker, S. (1986). 'Father–daughter sexual abuse: an emerging perspective'. *American Journal of Orthopsychiatry*, 56 (4), October 1986, 531–48.

Perlman, H. (1957). *Social Casework*. Chicago, University of Chicago Press.

Peters, J. J. (1976). 'Children who are victims of sexual assault and the psychology of offenders'. *American Journal of Psychotherapy*, 30 (3), 395–421.

Phillips, J. L. (1981). *Piaget's Theory: A Primer*. Salt Lake City, W. H. Freeman.

Pierce, B. (1987). 'Feminist view of child abuse', Letter to *Community Care*, 26 November 1987.

Pringle, K. (1988). 'Parents in training'. *Community Care*, 17 March 1988, 28–30.

Reich, J. W. and Gutierres, S. E. (1979). 'Escape/aggression incidence in sexually abused juvenile delinquents'. *Criminal Justice and Behaviour*, 6, 239–43.

Renvoize, J. (1982). *Incest: A Family Pattern*. London, Routledge & Kegan Paul.

Roberts, J. (1987). 'Fostering the sexually abused child'. *Adoption and Fostering*, vol. 10, no. 1.

Rush, F. (1980). *The Best Kept Secret*. New Jersey, Prentice-Hall.

Russell, D. (1983). 'The incidence and prevalence of intrafamilial sexual abuse of female children'. *Child Abuse and Neglect*, 7, 133–46.

Schechter, M. and Roberge, L. (1976). 'Child sexual abuse', in Helfer, R. and Kempe, C. H. (eds) (1976). *Child Abuse and Neglect: The Family and the Community*. Cambridge, MA, Ballinger.

Schultz, L. G. (1982). 'Child sexual abuse in historical perspective'. *Journal of Social Work and Human Sexuality*, vol. 1, nos 1 and 2, 21–35.

Sedney, M. A. and Brooks, B. (1984). 'Factors associated with a history of childhood sexual experience in a non-clinical female population'. *Journal of the American Academy of Child Psychiatry*, 23, 215–18.

Sgroi, S. (1982a). *Handbook of Clinical Intervention in Child Sexual Abuse*. Lexington, MA, Lexington Books.

Sgroi, S. (1982b). 'Family treatment of child sexual abuse'. *Journal of Social Work and Human Sexuality*, vol. 1, nos 1 and 2, 109–28.

Simmons, T. (1986). *Child Sexual Abuse: An Assessment Process*. NSPCC, Occasional Papers Series.

Steele, B. and Alexander, H. (1981). 'Long term effects of sexual abuse in childhood', in Mrazek, P. B. and Kempe, C. H. (1981) (eds). *Sexually Abused Children and Their Families*. Oxford, Pergamon.

Swiney, F. (1907). *The Bar of Isis*. London, C. W. Daniel.

Thomas, T. (1986). *The Police and Social Workers*. Aldershot, Gower.

Tufts New England Medical Centre, Division of Child Psychiatry (1984). 'Sexually exploited children: service and research project' (Final report for the office of Juvenile Justice and Delinquency Prevention. Washington DC. United States Department of Justice.) Quoted in Finkelhor, D. (1986). *A Source Book on Child Sexual Abuse*. Beverley Hills, CA, Sage.

Tunnard, J. (1983). 'Kept in the dark'. *Community Care*, 23 May 1983, 23–5.

Wakefield (1988). *West Yorkshire Police Initiative on Child Sexual Abuse Training Course*. January 1988.

Walrond-Skinner, S. (1976). *The Treatment of Natural Systems*. London, Routledge & Kegan Paul.

Warnock, E. (1987). 'Ethics, decision-making, and social policy'. *Community Care*. 5 November 1987.

Whitehouse, A. (1986). 'The anguish of the parent'. *Community Care*, 6 February 1986.

Woodcroft, E. (1988). 'Child sexual abuse and the law'. *Feminist Review*, no. 28, 122–30.

Wyre, R. (1987). *Working With Sex Abuse, Conference and Workshop Papers*. Oxford, Perry Publications.

Yorukoglu, A. and Kemph, J. P. (1966). 'Children not severely damaged by incest with a parent'. *Journal of American Academy of Child Psychiatry*, 5 (1), 111–24.

Index